The book is addressed to philosophers, political scientists
and general readers interested in a clear discussion of the
moral issues raised by terrorism.

Burleigh Taylor Wilkins is Professor of Philosophy at the
University of California at Santa Barbara. He is the author of
The Problem of Burke's Political Philosophy and *Has History
Any Meaning?*

POINTS OF CONFLICT

A new series from Routledge

The books in this series mark a new departure in academic publishing. Written by philosophers, or from a philosophical standpoint, their purpose is to probe beneath the shibboleths of day-to-day debate and controversy on important social and political topics. Common to all the authors is a view of the importance of the analytical skills of the professional thinker in reaching decisions on the large issues of our time. The books challenge the assumptions that lie behind the headlines and offer proposals, not always the expected ones, for action.

Also available:

Aids and the Good Society
Patricia Illingworth

Understanding War
W. B. Gallie

Terrorism and Collective Responsibility

Burleigh Taylor Wilkins

London and New York

First published 1992
by Routledge
11 New Fetter Lane, London EC4P 4EE

Simultaneously published in the USA and Canada
by Routledge,
a division of Routledge, Chapman and Hall Inc.
29 West 35th Street, New York, NY 10001

Phototypeset by Intype, London
Printed in Great Britain by
Clays Ltd, St Ives plc

British Library Cataloguing-in-Publication Data
Wilkins, Burleigh Taylor
  Terrorism and collective responsibility. –
  (Points of conflict)
  I. Title II. Series
  363.32

Library of Congress Cataloging-in-Publication Data
Wilkins, Burleigh Taylor
  Terrorism and collective responsibility / Burleigh
  Taylor Wilkins.
  p. cm. – (Points of conflict)
  1. Terrorism–Moral and ethical aspects. I. Title. II.
Series.
  HV6431.W55 1992
  303.6'25–dc20 91–16158

ISBN 0–415–07186–0
ISBN 0–415–04152-X (pbk.)

To Carla Cowgill Wilkins

Contents

Preface

I am indebted as always to my teachers and students. Two of my teachers deserve special mention for their work in areas relevant to this study: Joel Feinberg for his work in collective responsibility and rights, and Harold T. Parker for his work in administrative and military history. Joe White, Angelo Corlett, Victor Tam and Edmund Wall, although formally my students, were substantively my teachers as well.

Chapter 1, "Can terrorism be justified?", appeared in *Assent/Dissent*, edited by Joe White (Dubuque, 1984), and Chapter 2, "Terrorism and consequentialism," appeared in *The Journal of Value Inquiry* (1987). Although I have updated these chapters in several respects, they remain substantially as they were in their original form. Because the chapters of this book were written at different times over the past decade the reader will notice some differences in vocabulary, philosophical style, and emphasis, but none, I hope, in their overall consistency. This book is a study in applied ethics, so besides discussing the writings of other philosophers on the topics of terrorism and collective responsibility I have also commented on the works of some journalists familiar with these topics.

Introduction

Terrorists tend to be lumped together in the popular mind as men without conscience or as mad bombers, much as anarchists were regarded in the late nineteenth century. But in fact the anarchists who performed acts of violence at that time were motivated by the belief that the state was an instrument of oppression directed against the poor and the downtrodden; and terrorists also have their convictions, although these, unlike the anarchists', are not all of a piece. In our time terrorist acts have often been motivated by strongly held political beliefs of both the left and the right. Of course, the fact that an act is motivated by strongly held beliefs does not make it morally justifiable. Principled people and their actions can be, and sometimes are, quite horrible, but at least principled people and their actions differ, morally speaking, from criminals and their actions, a point which the popular press and former President Reagan often overlooked in their dismissal of terrorists as criminals. A more subtle way of refusing to take terrorism seriously from the moral point of view has been the effort of some psychologists to dismiss the actions of terrorists as those of alienated persons motivated not by strongly held beliefs but by something called 'narcissistic rage.' As a philosopher, I am not qualified to discuss 'narcissistic rage,' but the manner in which this hypothesis is employed is so patently reductionistic as to make me think that anyone who for whatever reason performs acts of violence may be suspect in the eyes of these psychologists.

One of the problems plaguing the discussion of terrorism is the lack of any agreed definition of the term; and some of the definitions we have are simply condemnations of terrorism.[1] Also, it would seem that there are at least as many definitions of terrorism as there are government agencies involved in dealing with it. Usually these definitions are skewed in the direction of favoring the activities, and budget, of the agency in question. Thus, for example, the American State Department's definition of terrorism emphasizes the political motivation of the terrorist while the FBI definition emphasizes the unlawful nature of terrorist violence. To compound the problem of defining terrorism, at least for philosophers, there is the issue of how important definitions are and how far they can take us even if they are accurate. Thus, for example, if it is true that justice consists in giving every man his due, this may not be much help in developing a theory of justice such as the one presented in John Rawls' *A Theory of Justice*.[2] However this methodological issue is resolved, some agreement on definition does seem required if only to ensure that we are talking about the same thing. I, therefore, shall propose, somewhat tentatively, a definition of terrorism which might be minimal enough to win acceptance.

Here is my definition: terrorism is the attempt to achieve political, social, economic, or religious change by the actual or threatened use of violence against persons or property. This definition has at least the advantage of not deciding in advance the question of whether the use of terrorism can ever be morally justifiable. The definition is also broad enough to include social, economic, or religious change among the possible objectives of terrorism. Since in point of fact most terrorist activities are directed not against persons but against property, a definition of terrorism, in order not to mislead, should perhaps acknowledge that it is not restricted to violence against persons. However, as stated, my definition appears too broad: wars and revolutions are also attempts to achieve political, social, economic, or religious change by violent means. I am not sure that on the level of definition terrorism can be distinguished from war and revolution, and terrorists, to justify their use of violence, frequently refer to themselves as being in a state of war. (I discuss the relationship of terrorism to war and revolution in Chapter 4 on terrorism and the just war tradition.) However, for my definition of terrorism several addenda may be helpful. The first is that the violence employed in terrorism is aimed partly at destabilizing the existing political or social order but mainly at publicizing the goals or the cause espoused by the terrorists. Hence the eagerness of terrorists to take credit for their acts of violence; indeed, whenever an act of violence is not 'claimed' by some terrorist organization this is presumptive evidence that the act in question was not committed by terrorists. (The bombing of Pan Am Flight 103 over Scotland may appear to be a counter-example. However, available evidence suggests that this bombing, while carried out by a terrorist organization, was done in return for a substantial payment from Iran, which sought revenge for the downing of an Iranian airbus by the American Navy during the Iran-Iraq War. Thus, a distinction between a terrorist act and an act of revenge suggests itself.) The second addendum is that often, though not always, terrorism is aimed at provoking extreme counter-measures which will help win public support for the terrorists and their cause, either because these counter-measures are seen as too harsh a retaliation against the terrorists or because they adversely affect the liberties or other interests of non-terrorists.

Wars and revolutions may be fought with an eye on their impact on public opinion, but they are rarely if ever fought in order to affect public opinion, and it would be a rare war or revolution in which the participants on either side hoped to provoke their adversaries into even harsher responses. Wars and revolutions are after all fought with victory in mind, but the case of terrorism is somewhat more complex. Terrorists, of course, hope to prevail eventually, but it is often said, correctly in my judgment, that terrorism is a weapon of the weak against the strong. Thus, while terrorism may lead to or accompany war or revolution, by itself it seems unable (at least thus far) to topple even the most insecure or precarious government. Only by appealing to the court of public opinion can terrorists hope to achieve their goals, and here they have been, in my judgment, very successful. Terrorism is, I believe, properly understood as an activity of not only the weak but the desperate. Terrorism is, after all, not a species of civil disobedience; while practitioners of civil disobedience may resort to civil disobedience after despairing of more conventional and legal methods of protest, they remain essentially optimistic concerning the fundamental soundness of the institutions of their community and the goodwill of their fellow citizens. The despair of terrorists is far more complete than that of the civilly disobedient, and the public opinion they are appealing to is often that of the 'world at large' rather than that of the community in which they reside. Theorists divide over whether civil disobedience admits of even the slightest amount of violence (Rawls is adamant that it does not[3]), but terrorism is, everyone would agree, essentially violent in its methods. Thus, the terrorist has to contend with the stigma attached to those who engage in violence. Some terrorists seek to overcome this stigma by their claim that they are actually in a state of war, but other terrorists, at least as interpreted by Albert Camus,[4] have taken upon themselves the burden of becoming moral outcasts or pariahs because they believe that attention simply must be paid to whatever wrong or injustice they are struggling against.

Being truly desperate, terrorists often take help in the form of arms, training, and moral support wherever they can find it. Sometimes the terrorists share the ideology of those who assist them and sometimes they do not. Now that the Cold War seems to have ended and some of the archives of the secret police of several Warsaw Pact nations have become public, it is clear that these nations did, as their critics alleged, actually give various kinds of aid to a number of terrorist organizations; and presumably these countries were acting with the approval of the Soviet Union, which may well have been providing some assistance of its own. It would have been surprising had they not done so, given their commitment to assist in so-called wars of national liberation. The crucial question was, however, whether the Soviet bloc was systematically and in a major way using terrorism to destabilize the Third World and western nations. Former President Jimmy Carter thought they were not, while President Ronald Reagan, Secretary of State Alexander Haig, and CIA Director William Casey thought they were. Interestingly, Haig's and Casey's opinions came not from American intelligence sources so much as from a book by Claire Sterling called *The Terror Network* (New York, 1981); one of the most intriguing stories in Bob Woodward's *Veil: The Secret Wars of the CIA 1981–87* is of Casey's efforts to force his subordinates in the CIA to support the conclusions arrived at by Sterling. However, the covert operators argued that Sterling's methodology was preposterous; and there were two contradictory draft opinions submitted, one by the CIA and the other by the Defense Intelligence Agency, concerning whether terrorism represented an international conspiracy. The CIA draft defined terrorism so narrowly that only 'pure' terrorists, those who engaged in violence for the sake of violence, were counted as terrorists, while the DIA draft defined terrorism so broadly as to include any violent action against constituted authority. Finally, it was agreed in conference that the Soviets were not the hidden hand behind international terrorism.[5] But even if they had been the hidden hand Casey was looking for, this would not have shown that terrorism was nothing but an instrument of the Soviet Union and its allies. In other words it would not have shown that terrorism was lacking in indigenous sources in the Third World and the West, or that there was not at least a disposition in some elements in these societies to respond favorably to Soviet entreaties. If I am correct, all reductionist accounts of terrorism, whether they are done in terms of the alleged psychological abnormalities of terrorists or in terms of the alleged use of terrorists by 'superpowers,' will be suspect; and, even if partially correct, these accounts will obscure the unique features which make terrorism what it is. In the final analysis, whatever our judgments may be, we cannot forget that terrorism is a struggle against what terrorists regard, rightly or wrongly, as injustice. If this were not so, it would be difficult to see what terrorists hope to gain by attracting public attention to their goals or cause.[6] Whatever they may think of their own actions, whether they see them as justified or as reprehensible, terrorists do believe in the rightness of their goals or cause, and this fact should be incorporated into any viable definition of terrorism.

My proposed definition of terrorism is now more complicated and it reads as follows: terrorism is the attempt to achieve political, social, economic, or religious change by the actual or threatened use of violence against persons or property; the violence employed in terrorism is aimed partly at destabilizing the existing political or social order, but mainly at publicizing the goals or cause espoused by the terrorists; often, though not always, terrorism is aimed at provoking extreme counter-measures which will win public support for the terrorists and their cause; terrorism will be perceived by its practitioners as an activity aimed at correcting grave injustices which otherwise would be allowed to stand.[7]

Here is what I attempt to do in Part 1 of this book. I consider and reject various arguments against terrorism, and conclude that terrorism can under certain circumstances be morally justifiable. This may initially seem to be an unacceptable thesis to those of us who are committed, as I am, to the values of liberal democracy. On the level of political theory I find myself in substantial agreement with Karl Popper's defense of the open society and John Rawls' theory of justice. However, I believe that Popper's dichotomy between reason and violence would be misread if it were understood as an exclusive disjunction, and that it would be a mistake to interpret him as saying that violence would under no circumstances be rational and defensible.[8] Rawls, instead of condemning all violence, can be read as saying that to the extent that we have recourse to violence we have lost faith in the justice of society's basic institutions or in society's willingness to rectify an unjust state of affairs. I believe that it is in societies where even the rudiments of the Popperian–Rawlsian ideal are conspicuously absent that we are most likely to find circumstances in which the possibility of a morally legitimate resort to violence exists.

In Chapter 1, 'Can terrorism be justified?,' I consider the deontologist's case against terrorism: terrorism involves the violation of the rights of innocent persons who may be killed or harmed, and even if no one is actually killed or harmed the threat of death or harm is a species of coercion, which is morally wrong. In this chapter, I consider the following questions: Can we ever justify inflicting violence upon innocent persons in circumstances other than self-defense? Will a 'justification' of terrorism succeed only if we shrink the notion of what is to count as innocence and/or extend the range of activities to be considered as self-defense? Is there such a thing as collective guilt, and if there is can it ever be used to justify violence against persons on the grounds that they are members of a certain community or group? In this chapter I argue that the persecution of the Jews in Nazi Germany is an example of collective guilt. I discuss Karl Jaspers' *The Question of German Guilt* and the four kinds of guilt he discovers: criminal guilt, political guilt, moral guilt, and 'metaphysical guilt.' To help make Jaspers more intelligible I employ the models of collective responsibility set forth by Joel Feinberg. I argue that there was enough complicity to involve many Germans in criminal guilt for what occurred, and that political inactivity on the part of the German people against what Hitler was doing made them morally guilty (as individuals) and politically guilty (as a nation). I argue that the persecution of the Jews by Nazi Germany would have justified terrorism as a kind of self-defense on the part of the Jews, but I argue that, to be justified, terrorism should be subject to certain constraints, the most important of which is that it should be selective wherever possible and should initially at least be directed only against the actual perpetrators of the injustice against those who are now considering the use of violence as a response.

In Chapter 2, 'Terrorism and consequentialism,' I consider arguments against terrorism developed by three philosophers who, broadly speaking, can be considered as consequentialists. R. M. Hare maintains that the possibility that terrorism might bring about a new state of affairs which people would like less than the present one is sufficient to dissuade a prospective terrorist from committing acts of terrorism. Kai Nielsen argues that the historical record shows terrorism and assassination to be ineffectual and even counter-productive as means of bringing about social and political change. Ted Honderich, although maintaining that there are facts about human suffering which would seem to justify violence aimed at altering these conditions, denies that we have the 'fairly precise judgments of probability' concerning the results of violence in specific cases which would provide us with 'overriding judgments' in support of it.

Against Hare I argue that the mere possibility that terrorism might fail to bring about the end state the terrorist seeks would not persuade the 'moral fanatic' not to engage in terrorism. Both Hare and Nielsen claim that 'history shows' that terrorism rarely if ever achieves the goals the terrorist seeks, but Hare does not even attempt to argue historically, and Nielsen, I maintain, fails to show that the historical record proves terrorism and assassination to be ineffectual or counter-productive. More seriously, Nielsen fails to show that Marx's theory of the class struggle, which he endorses, would rule out the use of terrorism or assassination. Against Honderich I argue that the facts about human suffering which he adduces might be sufficiently appalling, provided they can be shown to be the result of injustice, to justify terrorism even if we lack 'fairly precise judgments of probability' concerning the outcome of a resort to violence. I maintain that Honderich's requirement that we must have such judgments before any resort to violence can be justified is suspiciously *ad hoc*.

In Chapter 3, 'Violence and force,' I consider the following questions. Is violence different from force? Is violence necessarily a violation of a right? Is violence necessarily physical or can there be psychological and even institutional violence? I search for, and fail to find, the morally significant difference between force and violence which critics of violence allege exists. I argue that both force and violence may involve the violation of a right, but that violence does not necessarily or always involve the violation of any actual right. I acknowledge that violence can be physical, psychological, or institutional in character. As a methodological individualist, I can, however, think of the activities of institutions only in terms of activities by individuals who are their members and who act in accordance with their rules, norms, or standards. On this analysis, institutions do not, strictly speaking, do anything; only individuals possess causal efficacy. Thus, a violent institution would be, on this analysis, one with rules, norms, or standards which sanction or permit violent behavior by its members, behavior which results in harm, physical or otherwise, to other individuals. (By a harm I mean a set-back to an interest which is not necessarily a rights violation.) Having granted that there may be violent institutions, I argue, however, that not all institutional violence can justify a physically violent response by those who have suffered at the hands of (members of) violent institutions. First, to repeat an earlier point, not all violence is a violation of an actual right; and second, institutional violence, in cases where it does not involve physical violence, may involve psychological, economic, and social harms which, even when they are rights violations, may not be sufficiently severe to warrant a physically violent response. However, a cluster or a system of such rights violations may be sufficiently severe to warrant a physically violent response.

In Chapter 4, 'Innocence, just wars, and terrorism,' I return to the question of innocence. I note that there are several different senses of 'innocence,' and I examine the claim made by the terrorist George Habbash that in today's world there are no innocent persons. I explore some of the resemblances and differences between terrorism, war, and revolution, and I consider the just war tradition which has sought to lay down rules of conduct for combatants which will protect the safety of innocent parties. I argue that terrorism, while it may resemble war in some respects, is not necessarily a species of war and therefore may not be bound by the rules of combat laid down by the just war tradition.

In Part 2 I attempt a more detailed analysis of collective responsibility, and much of what I say here can be read separately from Part 1. I define collective responsibility as the responsibility of a group for some but not all of the activities of its members. Again, I look at collective responsibility from the point of view of a methodological individualist who believes that, while there are collective actions, these are the actions of individual members of a group acting in the name of or on behalf of the group to which they belong. Of course we say, for example, that the United States or the CIA did certain things, but 'rock bottom' explanations of social phenomena are, as J. W. N. Watkins insisted, to be found in statements about the actions, the beliefs, and the dispositions of individual persons.[9] Collective responsibility for these actions is, however, enormously complicated, as can be seen by considering the various models of collective responsibility provided by Joel Feinberg and discussed in Chapter 1. The principal authors I consider in Part 2 deny the adequacy of methodological individualism conceived of as a way of accounting for collective responsibility, and while it is fairly clear that they are using 'methodological individualism' in an extended sense, as having to do with the moral responsibility for collective actions, their challenge is well considered and worth detailed criticism. It seems that where human actions are concerned we are never going to find: (a) collectives that act apart from their individual members; or (b) isolated or atomic individuals who act entirely on their own, uninfluenced by some collective of which they are, or at least were at one time, members. The truth will be found, I think, to lie between these two extremes.

In Chapter 5, 'Responsibility for the My Lai Massacre,' I

consider the claim advanced by David Cooper that the responsibility for the My Lai Massacre is collective but non-distributive, and rests upon what he refers to as the US military system in Vietnam. I consider two examples advanced by Cooper of what he considers non-distributive responsibility, and I concede that, if we look at collectives or groups historically, there may be a moment or period in their history where we can say that a collective or a group may be sub-standard morally in its performance without its individual members being sub-standard in their individual conduct. However, I cast some doubt upon the importance of this, and I argue that in any case Cooper's two examples do not illuminate the responsibility of the US military system for the My Lai Massacre, in large part because he acknowledges that a substantial distribution of fault among individual members of the US military system is possible. I then consider his claim that this is still, properly speaking, a case of collective non-distributive responsibility because the collective responsibility in question is not exhausted by any distribution of fault among individual members of the US military system. In the process of criticizing Cooper I develop my own views on the collective responsibility for My Lai.

In Chapter 6, 'The responsibility of corporations,' I examine Larry May's important recent work, *The Morality of Groups.* Because the corporate environment is less coercive than a military system, especially in wartime, I find that corporate responsibility can be used to illuminate political responsibility as well. I discuss May's model of vicarious corporate negligence, and his claim that collective liability is not properly constructed as a species of strict liability, where strict liability is taken to mean that in cases of collective responsibility the contributory fault condition which is crucial to individual liability is either weakened or absent. I then discuss May's views on the punishment of corporations and corporate officers.

In Chapter 7, 'The distribution of liability,' I return to the topic of terrorism by considering the resemblances and differences between the punishment of corporations and corporate officers and the activities of terrorists against groups which they condemn. I make a distinction between the way in which courts punish corporations directly and their members only indirectly, and the way in which terrorists proceed directly against the members of some groups such as a nation state and only indirectly against such groups. Though the emphasis of this book is upon whether terrorism can be morally justifiable, I briefly consider the question of how terrorism should be dealt with in cases where terrorism is not justified.

Part 1

Terrorism

1 Can terrorism be justified?

Probably the most important division in moral philosophy is between consequentialists who believe that the rightness or wrongness of an action is determined by its contribution to an ideal end state such as the greatest happiness of the greatest number and deontologists who deny that this is so, at least in cases where the action in question would involve the violation of the rights of an individual or individuals. One of the few amusing aspects of the usually grim topic of terrorism is the way in which consequentialists such as R. M. Hare and Kai Nielsen seek to dissociate themselves from terrorism, treating it ever so gingerly as though fearful it might explode in their hands doing great harm to whatever variety of consequentialism they espouse.[1] Yet it seems to me plain enough that if there were good reasons for believing that terrorism would contribute to bringing about some ideal end state, then the consequentialist would be hard pressed to reject it as a morally legitimate means to that ideal end state. What then is wrong with terrorism if it cannot be condemned on consequentialist grounds? The deontologist's case against terrorism can be stated fairly simply: terrorism involves the violation of the rights of persons who may be killed or harmed; even if no one is actually killed or harmed by the terrorist, there is the threat of harm, and threats are a species of coercion, making people behave in ways that they would not otherwise choose; moreover, the persons who are, or maybe, the victims of terrorism are frequently not those whose conduct the terrorist wishes to affect.

Here Carl Wellman's distinction between the primary and the secondary targets of terrorism is useful, and his example of William Randolph Hearst (the primary target of the SLA) and Patricia Hearst (the secondary target) is well chosen.[2] No matter what William Randolph Hearst, a publisher of considerable influence and affluence, may have failed to do for the poor and downtrodden, and no matter how suitable from a certain ideological perspective he may have been as a target for terrorism, his daughter had done nothing to merit the treatment she received; and while her father undoubtedly suffered, this was mainly due to the suffering he believed his daughter might be experiencing. The kidnapping of William Randolph Hearst as a means of coercing the publisher into changing his policies and behavior must be regarded as significantly different from the kidnapping of his daughter as a means of coercing him into changing his policies and behavior. Should any person ever be coerced into doing what is morally right? The answer may well be yes, under certain circumstances. Should any person ever be coerced by threats of violence into doing what is morally right? Perhaps the answer will still be yes, but it seems far more doubtful that a person should be coerced into doing what is morally right by threats of violence against another individual. Even if Patricia Hearst had been a mature and articulate champion of the policies her father espoused there is still something especially repugnant about the manner in which she was used. And doesn't the Hearst example show exactly what is wrong with terrorism? Can't any member of a society be regarded as a potential hostage for the terrorist who seeks to coerce that society, or some significant segment thereof, into changing its ways?

It is important to remember that terrorism is not all of a piece, that it includes in addition to often highly publicized acts of violence against persons, acts which damage or destroy property and acts which disrupt communication or travel within a country. For the remainder of this chapter, however, I shall write only about acts of violence against persons; and if such acts are found to be, under certain circumstances, morally justifiable, this will not establish that terrorism in all its forms is morally justifiable. Still, on the assumption that violence against persons is the most significant form that terrorism can take, it would be extremely important if it could be shown, on grounds acceptable to the deontologist, that terrorism involving violence against persons may, under certain circumstances, be morally justifiable.

One other preliminary note needs to be made at this point: not every act that terrifies is to be counted as an act of terrorism. Wellman notwithstanding,[3] I cannot regard the rapist who coerces his victim into submission by threats of violence as a terrorist; nor for that matter can I regard the bombings of Hiroshima and Nagasaki as acts of terrorism, though undoubtedly they are properly regarded as terrifying acts aimed at coercing the Japanese into surrender. It seems to me that the rapist example somehow slips under the net of what any reasonable definition of terrorism would properly cover, while any definition which allowed the bombings of Hiroshima and Nagasaki to count as instances of terrorism would be too broad. The rape described in Wellman's example should not be considered as a terrorist act because typically it has objectives other than the alteration of social or political policy, which I see as being an essential aspect of terrorism. The bombings of Hiroshima and Nagasaki, while obviously intended by the American government to alter the policies of the Japanese government, seem for all the terror they involved more an act of war than of terrorism, which is not to say that the state of being at war precludes terrorist activities directed against the enemy. But only the choice of weaponry and the extent of the subsequent carnage make these bombings different from other, more routine bombings, though the choice of largely civilian targets may perhaps have placed them in the category of unjust acts of war.

One thing that makes terrorism of interest philosophically

is that it compels us to rethink from a somewhat different perspective the question of when, if ever, it is morally justifiable to do violence to another person. The traditional answers, while perhaps valid, will take us only so far. It is generally agreed that it is justifiable to do violence to another person in self-defense; some wars can be accommodated under the category of self-defense where this is construed in terms of a community of persons defending themselves against aggressors. It is also agreed, though less generally, that even violence against an innocent person can be justified in the name of self-defense, in cases where he or she is being used by an aggressor as a hostage or a shield. If in the Second World War the Japanese Army had dispersed crucial weapons and supplies throughout Hiroshima and Nagasaki, and if these weapons and supplies could only have been destroyed by attacks upon the entire cities, then we would, I think, be far less troubled about the moral legitimacy of our attacks upon them. (Here I assume that Japan was the aggressor.) But what about terrorism which seems to be no respector of innocence among persons, and which seems all too willing to sacrifice innocent lives as a means to social or political change? Can we fail to be shocked by the anarchist who justified tossing a bomb into a crowded café in Paris on the ground that there are no innocent bourgeois? (But would it be blasphemous to suggest that we might be somewhat less shocked had he deliberately chosen a café known to be frequented by captains of industry, whom he would have regarded as 'class enemies'?)

Though the victims of terrorist acts may be oppressors or aggressors or tyrants, or their collaborators, often they are not. Often they are innocent, at least as innocent as civilian populations in wartime. If we condemn unjust wars, or unjust acts committed in wartime, are we not also committed to condemning any terrorism in which violence, or the threat of violence, is inflicted upon innocent persons, except in those instances where they are being used as hostages or shields? Terrorism poses this problem: can we ever justify inflicting violence upon innocent persons in circumstances other than self-defense? Will a 'justification' of terrorism succeed only by shrinking the notion of what is to count as innocence and/or by extending the range of activities to be considered as self-defense? Is there such a thing as collective guilt, and if there is can it ever be used to justify acts of violence against persons on the ground that they are members of a certain community or group?

I believe that any adequate answer to the question of when, if ever, terrorism is justified must take into account the problem of collective guilt, which is surely one of the murkiest and least explored topics in moral philosophy and which, to my knowledge, has been entirely neglected by those who have written on terrorism. On the question of whether there is such a thing as collective guilt opinions differ: there are those who believe that we, all of us, are guilty of each and every wrong done by any human being, a view which Mohandas Gandhi seems to have held; there are those who believe that we can be guilty only of those wrongs which we have done in our individual capacity, a view which seems to be lurking just below the surface in the writings of some political libertarians; and there are those of us who are not satisfied with either of these extreme positions and who are attracted to, but disturbed by, the idea that guilt may be at least in some cases collective. If we are to make sense of the notion of collective guilt, I believe that solidarity in the sense of a shared or common interest is our best guide, and that the absence of wrongdoing by individuals who are nevertheless said to share in some collective guilt remains perhaps the biggest stumbling-block. The reason why humanity at large fails to be a satisfactory basis for pronouncements about collective guilt, except for the Mohandas Gandhis of this world, may be that the interests we share with humanity at large tend to be too slight or fragile, though this shows signs of changing. There are, however, communities of a less extensive and more tangible sort where shared or common interests are already conspicuously present: in families, in neighborhoods, in business or cultural institutions, in political states, and perhaps, if Marxists are correct on this point, in social and economic classes. Pride or shame in what is done in, by, or on behalf of such communities is probably the best phenomenological clue we have to locating the interests, and values we share with others. But where collective guilt is concerned we tend to balk at admitting to guilt for things done in, by, or on behalf of those communities whose interests and values we share, when as individuals we did not actively participate in the doing of the things in question. However, the tie between collective guilt and individual wrongdoing is not a conceptual one; and where collective guilt is concerned we can turn to the law for examples of liability without contributory fault. For example, even if personally entirely innocent of the offense, a bank officer may be held strictly liable for the wrongdoing of a bank employee; and a convincing rationale having to do with the vigilance which society can reasonably expect of bank officers in hiring and management procedures can be given for this practice. In addition, Joel Feinberg, the master taxonomist, has uncovered the following models of liability *with* fault: liability with a fault that is non-contributory; contributory group fault where the fault is collective and distributive; and contributory group fault where the fault is collective but not distributive.[4] I shall return shortly to these three models and to some of Feinberg's examples, but first I wish to consider an example of collective guilt which is, I believe, especially relevant to the question of whether terrorism can ever be justified.

I would suppose that in the history of imperialism, of racial and religious persecutions, and in the economic exploitation of one group by another there are numerous instances of collective guilt, but to my mind the clearest and most indisputable example in recent history is to be found in the persecution of the Jews in Nazi Germany. After the Second World War there was in fact an admission of guilt by the newly established West German government, and Chancellor Adenauer acknowledged an obligation on the part of the

German people to make moral and material amends for crimes perpetrated in the name of the German people; through treaty negotiations with Israel, West Germany agreed to pay out some 715 million dollars. As an example of penance this payment of reparations may be lacking somewhat in moral purity: Adenauer was under pressure from the American government and from world opinion, political considerations were obviously much involved, and the negotiations were between a new German government, perhaps even a new German state, and the newly created state of Israel. Nevertheless the example does fit, however awkwardly, the classic picture of guilt, confession, and repentance in the form of efforts to make amends through reparations.

But what exactly was the nature of the guilt involved in this case? Karl Jaspers in his brilliant book, *The Question of German Guilt*, distinguished four kinds of guilt: criminal guilt, political guilt, moral guilt, and what he called 'metaphysical guilt.' According to Jaspers, criminal guilt involved the violation of national and international laws and would be determined by trials of accused individuals in courts of law, including most conspicuously the Nuremberg trials; political guilt is necessarily collective and involves the liability of the German nation, a liability which, however, does not establish moral guilt; moral guilt concerns individuals who must answer in their own conscience the question of whether they lived in moral disguise, or with a false conscience, or in self-deception, or in a state of inactivity during the Hitler period; metaphysical guilt is defined as the lack of 'absolute solidarity with the human being as such' and found its expression in the feeling of guilt at being alive when one's Jewish neighbors were being taken away. Having made these distinctions, Jaspers warns against their misuse: political liability requires the German nation to make material reparations, but it does not establish moral guilt in the individual; criminal guilt, well, yes, but this affects only a few; moral guilt, here only my conscience can decide, and my conscience won't be too hard on me; metaphysical guilt, well, that's 'a crazy idea of some philosopher' – there's no such thing, or, at least as the philosopher himself admits, no one can charge me with it. Jaspers replies in part that there can be no radical separation of moral and political guilt, the reason for this being that there is no absolute division between politics and human existence: 'There is a sort of collective moral guilt in a people's way of life which I share as an individual, and from which grows political realities.'⁵ Jaspers then proceeds to examine various excuses having to do with historical and political circumstances, such as the weaknesses exhibited by the Allies who could surely have stopped Hitler at any of several points, the impotence of the German people in the face of the oppression and terrorism of the Nazi regime, and the ignorance of the German people concerning the cruelties going on in the concentration camps; and for reasons I haven't time to discuss he rejects them all.

Frequently in twentieth-century philosophy, analytic philosophy and existentialism have been at odds, existentialism having been created, or so it seems at times, to provide extravagant hypotheses to be demolished by analytic philosophy. This is not so in the present case, for Jaspers and Feinberg (who makes no mention of Jaspers) appear complementary to one another, and many of the distinctions Jaspers makes can be expressed in terms of a vocabulary familiar to analytic philosophers. Thus, the distinction between moral guilt and metaphysical guilt can be explained partially in terms of the difference between the failure to do one's duty and the failure to perform a supererogatory act: we have a duty of mutual aid to other human beings, to come to their assistance when they are hurt or in trouble, even at the price of considerable inconvenience to ourselves, but the duty of mutual aid does not require us to sacrifice our lives to save the life of another; and obviously nothing requires us to risk our lives in circumstances where we know that we cannot save the life of another. Still we can feel quite bad and even guilty in some circumstances where no one has come forward, even if we do not blame ourselves individually for having failed to do so. Metaphysical guilt, far from being a philosopher's invention, seems intelligible along the lines of Feinberg's model of contributory group fault, where the fault is collective but not distributive. Feinberg gives the example of the Jesse James train robbery: one armed man holds up an entire car full of passengers, and only heroes could have been expected to lead a self-sacrificial charge against the robber; however, the whole group could have resisted successfully, but fails to do so. On Feinberg's reading, while we cannot blame any individual passenger for failing to act, there is a flaw in the group. He writes, 'but a whole people can be blamed for not producing a hero when the times require it.'[6] Perhaps the metaphysical guilt which the individual German felt when he stood by helplessly as his Jewish neighbors were taken away, the feeling that he was somehow tainted just by remaining alive under such circumstances, reflects the failure of the community of which he is a member to have produced the hero or heroes which successful resistance to the Nazis would have required.

It seems correct to say that the moral guilt of the German people significantly resembles but does not entirely fit the model of liability with non-contributory fault and the model of contributory group fault where the fault is collective and distributive. Feinberg gives this example of liability with non-contributory fault: one man drinks heavily at a party, then drives home at normal (high) speeds, and injures a pedestrian; the claim that we are all guilty is a way of saying that this is a very common practice in which most of us participate, and that while the man who has caused the injury has done more harm than the rest of us it does not follow that he is more guilty or more at fault than the rest of us. For this model to fit exactly the German example most if not all Germans would have had to be anti-Semitic; then the Nazis would only have been doing what the other Germans would have done in similar circumstances, but this seems not to have been the case. Still the Nazis were successful in 'fanning the flames' of anti-Semitism, and it is difficult to see how the persecution of the Jews could have continued over the years without some considerable 'grassroots' support. Feinberg gives this example of contributory group fault where the fault is collective and distributive: all the members of a group or community are privy to a crime or tort as conspirators or accomplices or joint tortfeasers. Here it would be wrong to say that all Germans were privy to the crimes being committed by the Nazis, but surely many of them were. According to the criminal law, complicity in a crime takes a variety of forms and reflects varying degrees of participation: there are perpetrators, inciters, abettors, and protectors. Those who give refuge to the perpetrators, those who encourage and congratulate them, those who withhold knowledge of what the perpetrators have done, and those who are bribed into silence are all legally guilty of complicity. Here it should be noted that the post-war trials of Germans who were involved in the persecution of the Jews tended to be limited to actual perpetrators, and that their inciters, abettors, and protectors were largely ignored; had this not been the case, then the 'few' who were found criminally guilty would surely have been more numerous. Where moral guilt is concerned it is important to note that complicity extends beyond the limits of the law. Someone who sees that a crime is about to be committed, or is in process of being committed, but keeps silent simply because he or she doesn't wish to get involved may be morally guilty of complicity even if legally innocent. (Recent Good Samaritan laws requiring individuals to report a crime in progress may be seen as an attempt to bring the law into line with what many of us believe is already morally required.) Jaspers writes, 'We knew about concentration camps, though ignorant still of the cruelties going on there.'[7] This sounds very much like a radical version of moral complicity, implying not suspicion but knowledge of an elaborate crime continuing over many years, though 'we' remained ignorant of its full extent. Also, it is arguable that many individuals who advanced their careers with the assistance or approval of the Nazis in power were in effect allowing themselves to be bribed into silence. Thus, it would seem that the German people were morally guilty where the fault in question — complicity — was collective and distributive among many but not all Germans.

Concerning what Jaspers calls political guilt, this is collective and distributive in the fullest sense. Only those Germans who actually resisted the Nazis by completely severing their ties to the political community, and who renounced all benefits accruing from membership in such a community, would be exempt; and it is an interesting question whether, upon returning from exile or emerging from the underground to participate in the new post-war Germany, they would not then become retroactively politically guilty! It would seem that they could not, morally speaking, easily justify, say, a refusal to pay taxes which would go toward the payment of reparations to the Jews solely on the ground of their historical opposition to the Nazi regime; their return would indicate a moral commitment to sharing in the burdens and benefits of the community, even if they had once done all they could to prevent the persecution which gave rise to the political liability in question.

Where the issue of criminal guilt is concerned, I take partial exception to what Jaspers has to say. While he is explicit in linking moral and political guilt, with the German way of life as the connection, he is not so explicit in linking criminal guilt with moral and political guilt. Thus, on his analysis criminal guilt appears non-collective and distributed only among those individuals who actually committed crimes in violation of national or international law. While sensitive to moral complicity and its many subtle guises, Jaspers virtually ignores the criminal law and fails to call attention to the many forms that criminal complicity may take. Moreover, if moral and political inactivity in itself contributes to the commission of a crime, then those who are inactive may, morally at least, be held liable for the crime in question. This latter point seems implicit in Jaspers' own indictment, while discussing moral guilt, of political inactivity as a fault the post-war German conscience must confront and acknowledge. Indeed, in the final analysis Jaspers' account of the four kinds of guilt he considers turns out to be holistic and dynamic: by this I mean that he helps to make us aware of how the different kinds of guilt were interrelated, feeding upon one another and contributing to a collective guilt for both the persecution of the Jews and the origins of the Second World War. I think, though this is conjectural, that Jaspers may have regarded metaphysical guilt as being the most basic of the various kinds of guilt he examined; certainly he prompts us to consider whether all guilt might rest ultimately in the refusal to acknowledge human solidarity. What Jaspers did not develop was this idea: the political community or nation state stands as the fullest institutional expression of human solidarity we have to date, and yet it may serve to block even fuller expressions of that solidarity. This is obvious in the history of warfare among nation states, but it can receive an especially tragic expression when the nation state brings its power to bear against some of its own members. This is the first definition of terrorism given by one of our dictionaries: terrorism by a government against its people, or a segment of its people.

The persecution of the Jews by the Nazis was so heinous that, it seems to me, terrorism on the part of the Jews would have been a morally justifiable response, meeting terrorism with terrorism. What I have in mind is not terrorism thought of in terms of vengeance or even retribution but terrorism regarded as an instrument of self-defense on the part of the Jews. While Jews in Germany did to some extent resist their oppressors, they did not practice terrorism. Perhaps terrorism by the oppressed was an idea whose time had not come; perhaps the Jews did not want to 'sink to the level' of their persecutors; or perhaps there was a fear of making bad matters worse. Where sinking to the level of their oppressors is concerned, the Jews might have reasoned as follows: they were being persecuted because they were Jews, and if they practiced terrorism in turn, would they not be initiating violence, or threats of violence, against Germans because of their Germanness? There is, however, a crucial disanalogy between the two cases, which is sufficient in my judgment to overcome this objection. The Jews had done no wrong, and the effort to discredit them consisted of a tissue of lies: they had betrayed Germany in the First World War causing its defeat, they were responsible for Germany's post-war economic collapse, and so on. On the other hand, Germans were collectively guilty of the persecution of the Jews – thus, if Germans were the victims of violence, or threats of violence, by the Jews it would not have been because of their 'Germanness' but because of their collective guilt for the persecution of the Jews, for being Jews. As for making bad matters worse, perhaps one could find a point in the history of the persecution of the Jews and say that henceforth it would be difficult to see how anything could have worsened their plight. Perhaps terrorism aimed first against the Nazis and then against other Germans might at least have helped to focus German and especially world attention on what was happening in Germany. Even if terrorism by the Jews had done nothing to improve matters, striking out in self-defense is, I believe, a morally legitimate action on the part of anyone who has been condemned to death. State terrorism was being practiced against the Jews, terrorism not as a species of coercion but with the aim of the annihilation of the Jews. How much of what the Nazis were doing in this respect was actually sanctioned by German law remains a somewhat controversial topic, but surely whether legally or not the apparatus of the German state was being directed toward the extinction of the Jews. Under such circumstances Jews in Germany were in effect being driven into a Hobbesian state of nature, pursued by a Nazi Leviathan, and this is why I believe that terrorism was a morally acceptable option had the Jews elected to use it.[8]

In summary, my thesis is that in the case of the persecution of the Jews, reparations by the German government for crimes done in the name of the German people was a morally appropriate response *after* the harm was done, but that terrorism as an instrument of self-defense by the Jews would have been a morally appropriate response *while* the harm was in process of being inflicted upon them. But what does this example of a case where terrorism would have been morally justifiable actually show? There is a tendency among some commentators on the topics of terrorism and assassination to maintain that while some instances of terrorism or assassination might be justified, in the name of moral necessity, this is a far cry from our being able to arrive at a moral rule which would justify terrorism or assassination: the thought seems to be that exceptions to a moral rule do not provide the basis for a new moral rule.[9] There are some weighty metaphilosophical and methodological problems involved in all arguments of this kind which I shall, mercifully, not attempt to explore here. Instead, I shall conclude by proposing a rule for your consideration. There may be other rules which would justify terrorism, and the rule I shall propose is couched only in terms of sufficient conditions, although I believe that the first condition laid down by the rule I propose may well be a necessary condition which any justification of terrorism would have to satisfy. Here is the rule: terrorism is justified as a form of self-defense when: (1) all political and legal remedies have been exhausted or are inapplicable (as in emergencies where 'time is of the essence'); and (2) the terrorism will be directed against members of a community or group which is collectively guilty of violence aimed at those individuals who are now considering the use of terrorism as an instrument of self-defense, or at the community or group of which they are members. Perhaps there may be other acceptable moral rules which would justify the use of terrorism, for example in cases where an entire people have been dispossessed of their homeland, or where one part of a country is occupied by a foreign power which prevents its being reunited with the country of which it is historically and culturally a part, or where one economic class or one race systematically exploits another economic class or race. Here the issue would be whether dispossession, separation, or exploitation as contrasted to violence against persons is sufficient to warrant terrorism as a response, and whether the struggle to remedy the wrongs in question could be regarded as falling somehow within the category of self-defense. Perhaps rationales for terrorism which do not depend upon whether self-defense is involved might be constructed, but I shall not explore this possibility here; nor shall I consider whether terrorism in the absence of any collective guilt in the group toward which the terrorism is directed might somehow be justified.

Where the application of the moral rule I have proposed is concerned, I believe that the employment of terrorism against members of a community which is collectively guilty of violence should be subject to certain constraints in which moral and prudential considerations are interwoven. There is no reason why terrorism should necessarily be indiscriminate, and there are good reasons why it should not be. The picture given by the popular press, and R. M. Hare,[10] of the terrorist firing off an automatic weapon in a crowded airport misses the mark: most terrorists are in fact far more selective than this suggests, and even if they were not, there is nothing essential to terrorism which requires that its targets be randomly or indiscriminately selected. Here are the constraints I have in mind. First, the terrorism should be limited to the members of the community which is collectively guilty of violence. (It might be noted that the indiscriminate firing of a weapon in a crowded airport would be disqualified right off, on the ground that members of other communities, tourists and businessmen for example, commonly frequent such places.) Second, as far as possible terrorism should be confined to 'primary targets,' and where this is not possible the terrorist should pick a 'secondary target' who is as guilty or nearly as guilty, in the sense of being responsible for initiating or participating in the violence which can be said to have 'started it all' and which is continuing. An individual who simply shares the beliefs and attitudes of the 'primary target' would not be an acceptable 'secondary target.' (Also, the choice of a morally inappropriate 'secondary target' might backfire tactically in the sense of creating public sympathy for either or both of the targets involved − arguably, something like this may have happened in the Hearst case, which, of course, involved a terrorism different from the kind I am now considering.) Third, the terrorism in question should be directed initially at the perpetrators of violence and then at their accomplices in such a way as to reflect the part they played in the violence. If terrorism still fails to achieve its goal, the successful defense of the terrorists or the community or group to which they belong, then they should proceed to violence against those who, as individuals, are guilty of moral complicity in the violence in question. For example, the editors, the bankers, the university professors and the motion-picture makers who 'knew what was going on' – and were handsomely rewarded for their silence and acquiescence – should be the next in line. But what about members of the 'silent majority' who, it would seem, do no evil, see no evil and hear no evil, or if they do hear aren't really listening or dismiss what they hear as rumor? If the terrorists are seeking a change in the policies which have led to the violence directed against themselves or the community or group of which they are members, then perhaps the 'silent majority' was their ultimate addressee all along, i.e. the addressee whose attention they had sought vainly to get by legal or political means and which they now seek by violent means. Certainly it seems reasonable to suppose, again using the German example, that no systematic persecution of significant numbers of innocent persons can continue over long periods of time if the 'silent majority' is awakened from its lethargy or its preoccupation with the details of its daily existence. Terrorists can be pictured as saying, 'We demand your attention.' But what if they fail, in their campaign of violence against the perpetrators of violence and their criminal and moral accomplices, to awaken the conscience and the voice of the 'silent majority'? Then it would seem that the 'silent majority' itself would become tainted first with moral and perhaps eventually even with criminal complicity in the ongoing violence directed against the terrorists and the community or group they represent. Under these circumstances at least, some judicious, highly selective terrorism aimed at members of the 'silent majority' might become morally appropriate and tactically necessary, as a reminder that no one is safe until the injustice in question is ended.

I shall conclude by giving a brief, explicit statement of how what I have done above relates to the questions I posed earlier. First, can we ever justify inflicting violence upon innocent persons in circumstances other than self-defense? Here my justification of terrorism applies where those who are considering it as an option either have themselves been the actual or intended victims of violence, or are members of a community or group which has been the actual or intended victim of violence. Thus, the terrorism I defend is a species of self-defense, but may it involve inflicting violence upon innocent individuals? Here, the answer is a yes and a no. Yes, it may involve inflicting violence upon those who in their individual capacity may have done or intended no harm to the would-be terrorists or to the community or group to which they belong; but no, the individuals in question by virtue of their membership in the community or group which has done or threatened to do violence to the would-be terrorists or the community or group to which they belong are collectively guilty of the violence in question. (I shall discuss the distribution of liability over members of a group in Part Two.) Will my justification of terrorism succeed only by shrinking the notion of what is to count as innocence and/or by extending the range of activities to be considered as self-defense? The answer to the first part of this question is that no conceptual revision or change in the criteria for the use of the concepts we have is necessary: the concept of collective guilt is already in place in our moral vocabulary, and while my use of collective guilt as part of a justification of terrorism under certain circumstances may be original, I am not using the concept 'collective guilt' in any novel way, as my excursions into Feinberg and Jaspers show. The range of activities to be considered as legitimate self-defense may, however, be extended in the light of my justification of terrorism under certain circumstances. But if individuals and communities may

justifiably kill or fight wars in self-defense, I believe that terrorism may also under certain circumstances be considered a
legitimate instrument of self-defense. Of course, not all terrorism can be seen as involving self-defense, and I have said
nothing to justify any terrorism in which self-defense, and self-
defense against actual or intended violence, is not the central
moral consideration. Is there such a thing as collective guilt,
and if there is can it ever be used to justify acts of violence
against persons on the ground that they are members of a
certain community or group? Here, of course, my answer is
that there is such a thing as collective guilt, but that to justify
acts of violence against persons on the ground that they are
members of a certain community or group is permissible only
when 'membership in a certain community or group' is clearly
understood to be elliptical for 'membership in a certain community or group which has done or intended to do violence
against the would-be terrorists or the community or group to
which they belong.' In other words, it is not membership in
a particular community *per se* but membership in a community
or group which is collectively guilty of wrongdoing that is
morally relevant; to regard community membership otherwise
would involve a relapse into an unacceptable barbarism.

2 Terrorism and consequentialism

In the previous chapter I noted that consequentialists have tended to join in the condemnation of terrorism. While conceding that under some circumstances terrorism could perhaps be justified, consequentialists have quickly proceeded to assert that, of course, such circumstances are in fact rare or non-existent and that, given the world as we know it, terrorism cannot be justified. R. M. Hare, in a well-known essay on slavery,[1] has maintained that it is one of the virtues of consequentialism that its adherents have taken the trouble to determine what the harmful consequences of slavery actually are before rejecting it; but although Hare in his essay on terrorism has examined the immediate consequences of a single, hypothetical terrorist act, neither he nor any other consequentialist has examined the long-term consequences of a series of acts of terrorism, either real or hypothetical, which are interconnected and aimed at a common goal. Here, as elsewhere, what one might say on the micro-level of what an individual has done need not coincide with what one might say on the macro-level where a social practice is concerned. In this chapter I shall examine in some detail arguments against terrorism which have been presented by Hare, Kai Nielsen, and Ted Honderich, who, despite major differences among them, can all be considered as being in some sense consequentialists.

In his essay 'On terrorism' Hare commences by offering two distinctions: first, between nationalism and fanaticism; and second, between terrorism and revolution. The first distinction is roughly this: the prescriptions of the nationalist are not universalizable and cannot be counted as moral prescriptions, while those of the fanatic are universalizable and hence must be seen as moral prescriptions. By means of this distinction Hare seeks to dismiss terrorism of the nationalist variety while establishing that the terrorism of the fanatic at least merits serious consideration from the moral point of view. Hare's distinction turns upon his definition of nationalism as having to do with the self-interested pursuit of the interest of *any* group where such a group, like a self-interested individual, is not prepared to claim or do for other groups having 'precisely the same universal properties' (Hare's phrase) what it is prepared to claim or do for itself.[2] By contrast, fanaticism as defined by Hare is prepared to extend the claims it makes to all groups which have precisely the same universal properties as the individual group it happens to be defending. The second distinction Hare makes is between terrorism and revolution. He excludes 'the attempt by violence to depose a government in *coups d'état* and revolutions of the ordinary kind' from the category of terrorism. According to Hare, terrorism is engaged in when there is 'no immediate hope' of deposing the government; it may be considered a prelude to, but is not, revolution.[3]

I believe that Hare's two distinctions are seriously misleading. The result of his 'definitions' of nationalism and fanaticism is that the former ends up outside the pale of serious moral consideration, yet some reflection would show that what he has said about the fanatic could as easily be said of the nationalist. Surely it must come as a surprise to many enlightened nationalists to learn that they would deny that other nations, or groups, having 'precisely the same universal properties' as their own, would be entitled to claim or do what their nation or group is entitled to claim or do. Perhaps it would be even more astonishing to many terrorists to learn that they are not engaged in revolution or war. As I indicated in the Introduction, there may be some reasons to distinguish terrorism from revolution or war, and Hare is surely right in saying that terrorism may be (only) a prelude to a revolution. However, he overlooks the fact that terrorism may also occur during a revolution and may be an integral part of an ongoing revolution, and it may be very difficult to say where one activity leaves off and the other begins. Hare's claim that terrorism is engaged in when there is no 'immediate hope' of toppling a government reflects in a somewhat misleading way the fact that terrorism by itself seems unable to topple a government, but it would be false to say that terrorism under-taken as part of a revolution necessarily indicates the absence of any 'immediate hope' of success in the near future. Since all hope in so far as it is consciously, actively entertained may be considered 'immediate,' I assume that Hare in speaking of the 'immediate hope' of deposing a government means the hope of immediate success or success within a fairly short period of time. But surely even revolution cannot be linked that closely with the hope of immediate success or success within a fairly short period, nor can terrorism be defined by the absence of any such hope. Any human struggle may turn out to be a long, protracted affair in which hope can easily ebb and flow; accordingly, to use anything so mercurial as hope of immediate or near success to distinguish one kind of activity from another tends to be absurd. I shall have more to say about Hare's two distinctions, but here let us note their impact on discussions of terrorism. If Hare is correct, neither nationalism nor revolutionary terrorism can be construed as deserving serious consideration from the moral point of view, the first because it is solely self-interested and the second because, strictly speaking, there is no such thing. Nothing is said by Hare about non-political terrorism, which is religious, economic or cultural in its motivation, though I suspect he would dismiss the prescriptions of any such terrorism as being 'nationalistic' in his special sense of that term. An awful lot has been left out, and all that is left in seems to be the terrorism of the fanatic who, according to Hare's second definition, would seem to be lacking any hope of immediate success or success within a fairly short period.

It is small wonder that Hare's central example of terrorism turns out to be a terrorist 'killing a lot of people in an airport lounge with a submachine gun.' The consequences of his action are, according to Hare: (1) killing these people; (2) bereaving their families; (3) wounding others; (4) disrupting air travel; (5) causing governments and airlines to spend a lot of money on protecting against terrorism; (6) increasing taxes and the cost of air travel; and (7) helping, or so the terrorist thinks, to produce a state of affairs in which the cause he has embraced is likely to be advanced. In setting out this example, Hare does not tell us what the terrorist is doing in the airport in the first place. Nor are we told what other terrorists, if there are any, may be doing or planning to do – in short this is, so far as we know, a lone terrorist. He is not in the airport as part of any revolution or *coup d'état*, there is no 'immediate hope' of deposing the government, and so on. And in the example we are not told *who* is being shot, though presumably it is not the head of state or a political figure upon whom the government depends for its existence, for that would bring the activity of the terrorist closer than Hare would admit to being a part of a revolution or *coup d'état*.[4]

Hare then proceeds to ask whether history shows that terrorism achieves the good results hoped for by its perpetrator. His answer is that history shows that this has 'very seldom' been the case and that terrorism usually fails to achieve a 'balance of good' that would justify the suffering it causes. He then introduces what in effect turns out to be a very complicated hypothetical. Suppose that terrorism, after causing much suffering, brings about the state of affairs the terrorist seeks, say a classless society, and suppose the people in that society do not like it 'nearly as much as the present state of affairs,' can the moral fanatic justify the terrorism which has brought about the new state of affairs? Hare answers that he cannot, and thus the only morally defensible variety of terrorism, that of the moral fanatic, is shown to be ultimately unacceptable.

Hare allows that it is 'possible to dream up cases in which acts of terrorism could be justified on utilitarian grounds.' He acknowledges, by way of example, that some of the acts of the French Resistance against the Germans could be so justified, but he attaches no importance to this concession; and it is doubtful whether his example is, strictly speaking, one of a terrorism which he would regard as meriting moral consideration, i.e. terrorism of the moral fanatic as contrasted with that of the nationalist. For that matter so-called acts of terrorism by the Resistance in wartime might turn out, again strictly speaking, not to be examples of terrorism at all. Here it is important to recall Hare's distinction between terrorism and revolution, and to consider the possibility that acts of violence in wartime, like acts of violence in a revolution, might not even be acts of terrorism in Hare's technical sense.[5]

Let us look more closely at Hare's example of the terrorist in the airport lounge. On my interpretation Hare is saying that the prescription of the moral fanatic is universalizable, but that universalizability is only a necessary and not a sufficient condition for a prescription's being morally acceptable. According to Hare, considerations of utility must be taken into account and, in his view, the example of the terrorist in the airport lounge shows that more negative than positive utility will result from his action even if it does help to bring about the state of affairs he desires. Where the example of the terrorist in the airport lounge is concerned I believe that the question of time is crucial. If Hare is correct, the terrorist has no 'immediate hope' of realizing his ultimate objectives, and in any case it seems likely that the people who live to see the results of his activities may not be the same as those who witnessed what he did or read about it in the morning paper. This difference may prove important. It would seem that the difficulties which plague all interpersonal comparisons of utility might prove even more troublesome when comparisons across generations are attempted. Or perhaps the only relevant question here would be the following: using Hare's example, do we find that people who live in the new classless society like it as much as they would have liked the state of affairs which existed when the terrorist entered the airport lounge? To simplify matters, however, let us forego all questions of comparison with previous states of affairs, and let us suppose that the new classless society is just not liked at all. Under these circumstances, the terrorist's action in the airport lounge would clearly be unacceptable from a consequentialist point of view, as Hare has maintained. However, this approach to the problem succeeds only by neglecting what the terrorist may have had in his mind at the time of his action. Surely the terrorist in thinking that his action would help to produce the state of affairs he desired did not also entertain the belief, or possess the knowledge, that this state of affairs would turn out to be odious or intolerable to those who experienced it. Had he held such a belief, or possessed such knowledge, and still gone ahead with his action, he would have crossed the line from moral fanaticism to a monstrous uncaring about both the present and future harms he was inflicting upon others. And in fact it is hard to imagine anything more likely to prevent the terrorist from firing off his weapon than such a belief or piece of knowledge. (He may, of course, think that people will have to be re-educated in some respects before they can fully enjoy the new classless society, but what we are imagining here is the failure of any efforts at re-education, a failure he believes or knows will occur.)

The upshot of the above is that Hare's question, if it is to be taken seriously, has to be rephrased as follows. Suppose that terrorism does help to bring about the classless society, but suppose further that it is possible that people may not like that society, can the moral fanatic justify an act of terrorism such as firing a submachine gun and killing people in an airport lounge? The answer to this question is that it depends upon whether the moral fanatic, *at the time* that he is considering whether such an act can be justified, has good reasons for believing that people in the new classless society will not like it. What might count as a good reason? Perhaps evidence

that there will be a lower standard of living or a boring uni-
formity of taste and opinion. In any case, the mere possibility,
unsupported by these or other reasons, that the new classless
society may prove disappointing to those who experience it
is not going to persuade the moral fanatic that terrorism
cannot be justified. Hare, of course, would reply that there
are good reasons for taking possibility seriously in this case,
but these reasons turn out to be historical. History, according
to Hare, shows that terrorism 'very seldom' yields a balance
of good, but for all of his insistence upon the importance of
historical facts in moral disputations of this kind he adduces
no concrete, historical examples of what he would consider
as unsuccessful acts of terrorism. Nor does Hare give us reason
to believe that the future will be like the alleged past where
terrorism is concerned; perhaps the future will be, more and
more frequently, like that part of the past where terrorism
may have yielded a balance of good – notice that Hare says
terrorism has 'very seldom' yielded a balance of good, not
that it never has. I would suppose that the people of Algeria
and Kenya would say that terrorism, which in their countries
helped to bring about political independence, has created a
balance of good, and where the IRA and the PLO are concerned it is too soon to speculate what the so-called verdict
of history will be. Perhaps Hare might maintain that terrorism
associated with wars of national independence cannot be considered as morally defensible, given his strictures against
nationalism, or else he might say of nationalistic terrorism
what he has said about revolutionary terrorism, namely that
it is not, strictly speaking, terrorism at all, but then we are left
with the terrorism of isolated individuals or gangs such as
the Baader-Meinhof gang in West Germany for our principal
examples. These may be grist to Hare's mill, but they are
examples of a terrorism that fails to achieve its goals, not of
a terrorism which succeeds in bringing about a new social
order only to have this order condemned by those who
experience it.

If one takes seriously Hare's distinctions between nationalism and fanaticism and between terrorism and revolution, the result will be that the 'lessons of history' turn out to be very meager indeed. I imagine that readers of 'On terrorism' have chafed throughout at the way in which these distinctions have restricted and possibly distorted Hare's treatment of terrorism. Perhaps they have suspected that Hare's definition of nationalism was not, as philosophers say, a 'real definition' but a stipulative one aimed at disposing of nationalism as merely self-interested, hence involving prescriptions which cannot be universalized. A moment's reflection would suggest that enlightened nationalists would support the self-determination of all nations, and self-determination would seem to be a viable candidate for universalizability. But what about unenlightened nationalists who want their nation to rule the world or some part thereof simply because their nation will benefit if it does. If Hare is correct about universalizability, this is the kind of nationalism that cannot be taken seriously morally; but having distinguished between two kinds of nationalism, we need not attempt to answer the question of which kind is more typical historically. Rather, the relevant question is now whether terrorism on behalf of enlightened nationalism could be morally justified from the consequentialist point of view. If there are historical examples where terrorism has yielded a balance of good, then it would seem that the consequentialist would be forced to admit that there are good reasons for accepting terrorism. And, of course, not all consequentialists are committed to accepting universalizability as a necessary condition for moral prescriptions: those consequentialists who do not accept Hare's position on universalizability could presumably accept any prescriptions (including those made by unenlightened nationalists) which are likely to yield a balance of good.

In 'On terrorism' Hare imagines himself in a dialogue with the moral fanatic, a dialogue he is confident he can win. But imagine a dialogue in which the moral fanatic asks the questions, confident that *he* can win. Suppose, the moral fanatic might say, that in Hare's airport example conditions (1) through (6) obtain (see p. 36), cannot the possibility that terrorism might help to bring about the new social order sought by the terrorist, and the further possibility that this new social order will prove very satisfying to those who experience it, provide a justification of terrorism? This, I believe, is the ultimate nightmare question which all 'liberals' (those committed, as Hare is, to orderly social change through democratic, institutional procedures) must confront regardless of whether they accept any variety of consequentialism. And if the moral fanatic persuades us that terrorism will help to bring about a new social order which will be enjoyed by those who experience it, or will be preferred over the current one, if in other words the new social order seems likely to yield a balance of good, then I fail to see how one who reasons consequentially as Hare does could avoid capitulating to the moral fanatic.[6]

Following, as he puts it, in the tradition of Marx and Lenin, Kai Nielsen condemns terrorism and assassination on what are essentially consequentialist grounds. It is not, Nielsen maintains, the case that terrorism and assassination can never be justified, but it is usually the case that they are ineffectual and even counter-productive means to the end of social and political change. Nielsen writes that

> generally speaking, history is not made by individuals and that since this is so, it is rarely the case that the elimination of individuals will change anything in any substantial and important way. Rather the resort to terrorism is usually a sign of political weakness and sterility.[7]

As evidence that the elimination of individuals rarely makes a significant difference, he cites the assassination of Robert Kennedy. While conceding that Kennedy, had he become president, could have increased welfare measures and enhanced 'Black Capitalism' and that he probably would have ended the Vietnam War in a reasonably short time, Nielsen maintains that Kennedy would not have lessened racism in the United States, and that the end of the war would not have meant a pullback from American imperialism but simply a change in tactics. Thus if Nielsen is correct, we are to believe that Kennedy's assassination made little difference over all.[8]

If you argue as Nielsen does from the point of view of the inevitability of socialism, then of course a policy that, for example, enhances Black Capitalism will seem at best a noble anachronism, but I lack, and do not envy, a moral perspective which fails to see the question of whether the Vietnam War might have ended a few years sooner as being of any ultimate significance. Racism and imperialism go undefined in Nielsen's essay, but if the Vietnam War is taken as an instance of American imperialism, then I cannot see how the end of that war is not to be counted as a significant pullback from it. Surely the retrenchment which dominated American foreign policy for nearly a decade following the Vietnam débâcle was a pullback, unless this is taken to mean nothing less than the total cessation of any American political and economic involvement in the affairs of other nations.

In discussions of terrorism and assassination one's choice of examples is obviously crucial, especially for the consequentialist. Critics of terrorism and assassination prefer to choose examples where these actions fail to achieve the results sought by their perpetrators, and the implication is that there is something in the complex web of history which makes such failures virtually inevitable. But these critics forget that the most important assassination of the twentieth century, that of Archduke Ferdinand, achieved exactly the goal sought by the perpetrators, namely the liberation of Serbia from the Austro-Hungarian Empire. My case against Nielsen turns, however, upon something more than factual arguments for or against the efficacy of political assassination or terrorism.

Marxist-Leninist theory is, of course, revolutionary, and it is difficult to see how a revolutionary could, generally speaking, condemn terrorism and assassination. Since a Marxist-Leninist revolutionary must be prepared to do harm not only to property but to persons where necessary, Nielsen's quarrel with

terrorists and assassins can only be about what is 'necessary.'
Since Marxist theory is notoriously vague as to exactly when
a society has reached the point of being ripe for revolution,
I suspect that the charge of *adventurism*, of not following
the dictates of scientific socialism, can only be an *ad hoc*
condemnation of policies one happens to disapprove of, or
of revolutionary activities which have failed. (And I myself am
inclined to look upon Lenin as an adventurist who happened
to succeed in large measure because of the disastrous impact
of the First World War upon Russia.) Consequentialists who
espouse revolution will, I think, have great difficulty in dissoci-
ating themselves from terrorism and assassination. It is, after
all, no accident that the Red Brigade in Italy calls itself Red,
and no accident that considerable economic support for international terrorism seems to have come from the Soviet Union,
which is not known to invest in causes it regards as afflicted by
political weakness and sterility. And indeed Nielsen's phrase
'political weakness and sterility' is ambiguous: of course the
Red Brigade is politically weak in the sense that it could not
win an election, or could not directly influence government
policy in Italy as, for example, labor unions or the Vatican
might, but it is not politically weak or sterile in that it has
forced the government to spend time and energy in pursuit
of the Red Brigade that might better have been spent in other
areas. More importantly, the Red Brigade has gained publicity
for its cause, always an important objective of the terrorist. If
we were to distinguish, as Hare does, between terrorism and
revolution, then terrorism, and assassination, could still be
regarded as means to an eventual revolution, even if they do
not, as Nielsen might argue, constitute an actual revolution.
And once the revolution is underway, might not terrorism and
assassination become an integral part of it? So far as I can
determine, there is nothing in Marx's theory which would rule
this out. What Marx sees as being 'historically necessary' is
that there will come a moment in the history of capitalism
when it will be overthrown by the forces of socialism, but the
question of how it will be overthrown seems entirely open-

ended where the possible use of terrorism and assassination is concerned.

Of the three consequentialists I am considering, only Ted Honderich appears sympathetic to terrorism. There are, he tells us, 'facts which overwhelm any arguments about political obligation, and any residue of them. There are facts which stand in the way of our thinking that violence only rarely raises conflicts between moral necessities.'[9] He then proceeds to provide examples of such facts: (1) facts to do with differences in the average life expectancy in the less developed countries (forty-two years) and the economically developed countries (seventy-one years), a difference so great as to be *like a species difference*;[10] (2) facts to do with distributions of wealth and income within the more and less economically developed countries. Such facts are, Honderich acknowledges, difficult to summarize, but he believes they point to great concentrations of wealth and income within the economically developed countries, and to great discrepancies between the wealth and income of the more and less economically developed countries.

The facts as presented by Honderich seem appalling, and one expects his presentation of them to be followed by an eloquent justification of terrorism as a remedy of the injustices which they appear to document. However, this is not the case. Honderich thinks that a justification of terrorism would require us to have 'fairly precise judgments of probability' concerning the consequences which would result from violence, and these cannot usually be made with confidence.[11] Thus, we cannot make what Honderich calls 'overriding judgments about violence.' Honderich, however, rejects the notion usually associated with 'conservatism,' that uncertainty about the consequences of actions justifies our doing nothing, so he proposes that we can make 'lesser judgments' which are 'of some value as guides to action.'[12] However, these lesser judgments as elaborated by Honderich appear somewhat tame: he believes, for example, that the treatment accorded to violent movements should differ from one movement to another; and he also believes that when governments can rectify the circumstances of misery and fail to do so, this '*will be a recommendation of much violence.*'[13] What Honderich seems to be saying is that there may be good but not always sufficient reasons for violence and terrorism. This is how I interpret his distinction between 'overriding' and 'lesser judgments,' but what he fails to provide is any account of what would take good reasons for violence over the threshold, as it were, to become sufficient reasons for violence. And given what he says about the lack of fairly precise judgments of probability and why this is crucial, I am at a loss as to how on his analysis the actual use of violence could be justified. Unlike the conservative, Honderich would like to do *something*, but uncertainty about the consequences of our actions seems to stymie him, just as the conservative might hope it would.

I want to backtrack to the very beginning of Honderich's argument. The first mistake he makes is in his claim that the facts he calls our attention to 'overwhelm' any arguments about political obligation. In a rhetorical or practical sense some facts may interrupt or silence the process of arguing, but it is hard to see how facts, even facts about human suffering, can overwhelm the contents of the arguments themselves. The content of an argument about political obligation has to do with the circumstances, if any, under which we ought to obey the law, while facts of the sort adduced by Honderich can at the most tell us whether the circumstances specified in a theory of political obligation actually obtain in concrete situations. To attach more significance than this to factual considerations would amount to saying that they can by themselves determine whether there is an obligation to obey the law, and this would seem to violate the 'is' – 'ought' distinction which I for one wish to maintain. What Honderich has done in effect is to call our attention to the absence of a satisfactory general theory of political obligation, but this has to do with the present state of political philosophy and nothing to do with factual surveys of income distribution and life expectancy.

Despite the moral urgency and eloquence which attend his presentation of the facts, Honderich does surprisingly little to interpret them. Even the most elementary methodology would involve something like the application of J. S. Mill's Method of Agreement and Difference to the facts Honderich presents. For example, there was a time in the history of the US when the average life expectancy was no more than forty-two years. Let us say that this was roughly a hundred years ago. Now any comparison of the sort Honderich makes between the current life expectancy in developed and less developed countries could not, I think, be fully understood without some knowledge of what the average life expectancy was a hundred years ago in those countries where it is currently forty-two years. Has the life expectancy in these countries risen or fallen? And why has it risen in the US? Because of economic development? Or because of advances in medicine? And do these advances in medicine depend upon our having become more economically developed? In the case of less developed countries, the moral significance of the facts Honderich cites would in my judgment vary enormously if the average life expectancy there has fallen or risen significantly. If it has fallen, is this because of things the economically developed countries have done to the less developed countries (robbing them of their resources, or thwarting their industrialization, for example)? If the life expectancy in less developed countries has risen, is this in any way because of things the developed countries have done for them (teaching child care and hygiene, or providing famine relief, for example)? Suppose the life expectancy in the less developed countries has actually increased at a greater percentage than in the economically developed countries. Would the developed countries still be to blame morally, or as much to blame, because the absolute difference in the average life expectancy is still so great?

I wish now to raise briefly two issues which go entirely neglected by Honderich. First, there is the question of whether the facts he cites support 'lesser judgments' favoring violence by the 'oppressed' or favoring aid, or more aid, by the 'oppressors.' Second, while it seems reasonable to suppose that some of the factual discrepancies Honderich notes involve human-made inequities instead of 'natural injustices,' it is by no means clear, as Honderich apparently assumes, that this is true of all or even most of them. It seems equally reasonable to suppose that at least some of these factual discrepancies arise from 'natural injustices,' i.e. those misfortunes, be they absolute or relative, which overtake our fellow men and are not the result of any wrongdoing on our part. I believe, as I imagine Honderich would, that there is a duty of mutual aid where 'natural injustices' occur, and that this duty extends not merely from individual to individual but from community to community. But whether there is such a duty and if so what it requires of us in concrete situations is surely one of the most hotly contested topics in the theory of distributive justice.

My final objection to Honderich is this: if I were considering performing an act or acts of violence I would take a hard look at his claim that we cannot, at least usually, have fairly precise judgments of probability and that without these judgments as to the consequences of violence, there can be no overriding judgments about violence. This claim seems suspiciously *ad hoc*. Is there something special about acts of violence which makes them different from other acts where judgments concerning their consequences are concerned? We frequently do many things where the outcome is uncertain, without being inhibited by the lack of fairly precise judgments of probability. It seems to me that, whether it is done rationally or not, most of the world's decision making gets done in that vast, gray area which lies between William James' 'leap in the dark' and Honderich's decisions based upon fairly precise estimates of probability; moreover, I believe that the often irreversible harm to persons or property which violence involves does not *by itself* justify our requiring so much more information about probable outcomes in the case of violence than in the case of some other kinds of activities. Indeed, if the facts cited by

Honderich are as terrible as he thinks they are, then they might prompt a prospective terrorist to reason that *any* chance of altering them is worth the risk of failure and the near certainty of harm to persons or property that violence involves. Canons of rationality being what they are (or are not), I do not see how we could condemn terrorists for acting irrationally just because they lack the fairly precise judgments of probability Honderich would require. If the facts cited by Honderich are as they are because certain elements have taken unfair advantage of others in a society, or one society has taken unfair advantage of another society, then perhaps exploited people could be justified in using violence aimed at rectifying matters independently of whether they have reliable probability calculations which indicate that their chances of success are very high.

Once again I am forced to reach essentially the same conclusion: consequentialist arguments against terrorism have failed. Although I have done nothing to demonstrate that consequentialist arguments for terrorism could succeed where those against it have failed, common sense suggests that consequentialism might justify acts of terrorism under some circumstances. Indeed, it is hard to imagine any action which consequentialism could not justify, given appropriate circumstances. Consequentialists generally acknowledge this, but then proceed to argue that such circumstances rarely if ever obtain in the real world. However, in the case of terrorism this seems a difficult line to take, especially if the real world is as hellish for so many of its inhabitants as Honderich's facts would suggest. From a strictly consequentialist point of view it would seem that where human suffering is concerned the additional suffering caused by terrorism might be but a drop in the bucket, a drop which would seem justifiable if there were any chance at all that it might alleviate the wider human suffering to which it is a reaction.

3 Violence and force

Hare has remarked in 'On terrorism,' that we all know what terrorism is, but although this seems doubtful the connection between terrorism and the threatened or actual use of violence seems clear enough. Presumably, if we do not all know what terrorism is, we all know what violence is. But here, too, what we think we know in our precritical or preanalytical moments may turn out to be simplistic or even erroneous when we come to consider the following questions. Is violence different from force and, if so, how? Is violence necessarily a violation of a right? Is violence always or necessarily physical or can there be psychological violence and even institutional violence? In what follows I shall be concerned with violence and force conceived of as social phenomena, and nothing I say will have any direct bearing upon them as natural phenomena, e.g. the violence of a storm or the force of an earthquake.

Most philosophers seem to agree that there is some difference worth attending to between violence and force, but it may prove difficult to capture. If a drowning swimmer, all the while struggling hysterically to escape, is dragged to shore by a lifeguard, we would perhaps be inclined to say that force has been used but that no violence has occurred. But what if the lifeguard strikes the swimmer to subdue him so that he may be brought safely ashore? Here it would seem that violence has after all been done to the swimmer: see the bruise on his forehead or chin, we might say. But it may seem odd to have the difference between force and violence turn upon whether a person has been held tightly against his wishes or has been struck, especially when in both cases the object has been to subdue him in order to save his life. Would it make a difference if the swimmer were deliberately attempting to swim away from shore, if he were attempting suicide by drowning? Or would it make a difference if the swimmer was attacking another swimmer, and the lifeguard was attempting to prevent this? Would the example be significantly altered if the lifeguard was replaced by an ordinary person without any official standing?

Perhaps in our search for clear examples of force we might turn to cases of coercion, where physical force is not threatened. A wife who attempts to make her husband attend a party by threat of withholding sexual favors may be said, if she succeeds, to have forced her husband to accompany her, but has she used force? Perhaps, but then there are forceful arguments and forceful personalities, where surely we do not want to say that force has been used. The 'force of an argument' would seem to lie at the opposite pole from any actual use of force, and forceful personalities usually turn out to be simply persuasive or charismatic individuals who are able to carry the day without the use of any force. In these two cases it seems metaphorical to speak of force at all. Let us return to coercion. A man coerces another into betraying government secrets by threatening to reveal that he is a homosexual. Here we may be more inclined than in the earlier husband/wife example to say that force has been used, but what makes the difference except perhaps the seriousness of the respective sanctions? Is it that force is simply out of place in what may be only a bedroom farce but seems somehow to belong in cases where the threat involves public scandal or disgrace? And, of course, coercion may also be involved in cases where the use of physical force is threatened either by individual agents acting in their individual capacities or by representatives of the 'coercive power' of the state or community. Where the relationship between force and coercion is concerned one interesting feature should be noted. Although it is perfectly natural in cases of coercion to speak of someone being forced to do something by threats of various sorts, cases of coercion have in common one feature which may seem somewhat puzzling: an agent may refuse to be coerced by a threat, in which case the person attempting to coerce him must usually decide whether or not to carry out the threat in question. (I say usually but not always because sometimes a coercer may already have set in motion a process which will automatically result in harm to an agent who refuses to do his bidding; and even the coercer may now be powerless to reverse or stop that process.) Although coercion appears to be necessarily related to force, there can, of course, be force where there is no coercion. A coercer seeks to make 'an offer you can't refuse,' usually between two unpalatable alternatives neither of which an agent would choose under ordinary circumstances; but even in the strongest, most reprehensible case of coercion one can of course refuse, provided one is willing 'to pay the price.' Force need not be that way at all, hence the difference between simply being shot and robbed and the demand made at gunpoint that you surrender your wallet. However, the above discussion of coercion shows that not all force is physical; indeed some philosophers, overly impressed by the fact that a threat to use physical force may never be carried out, have wrongly concluded that the only force involved in coercion is psychological, and is to be understood in terms of the fear a coercer engenders in the party he or she is seeking to coerce.

The significance of the relationship between force and violence begins to emerge more fully when we consider the claim that violence may be physical, psychological, and even institutional.[1] Here it becomes clear that a large part of what is going on in attempts to differentiate force from violence turns upon whether there is some moral difference between the two. According to 'conservatives,' the police use force, but criminals use violence. But, 'radicals' reply, there are forms of violence other than the sort employed by criminals. There may be psychological or institutional violence, and the police in using force may be protecting a racial or political system which perpetrates psychological or institutional violence against persons, e.g. members of racial or religious minorities. Thus, 'radicals' may argue, physical violence when used by social or political activists against such a system may be justified; or 'radicals' might prefer to say that under these circumstances, what we actually have is the use of morally justified force against the morally unjustified though perhaps legal use of force by the police or other defenders of a repressive system or establishment. What the 'conservatives' and 'radicals' have in common is the belief that violence necessarily involves the violation of a right or rights, but I shall argue that this belief is mistaken.

Is it true that police use force but criminals use violence? Certainly a newspaper headline about 'police violence' would capture our attention more readily than one which speaks of the police using force: 'police violence' suggests that they have exceeded the bounds of their legitimate authority, have run amok and engaged in a misapplication of their powers. Here we have, I believe, encountered a significant point about one kind of force and its relation to political and legal authority. Usually, if not always, a sovereign political state reserves to itself a monopoly on the use of physical force within its boundaries or jurisdiction, and if there are circumstances, for example involving self-defense, in which the state allows individuals to employ physical force on their own behalf, it is the state which will specify what those circumstances are and what amount or degree of physical force individual persons will be permitted to employ. But in all but the most authoritarian (and capricious) states there are also limitations upon the amount or degree of physical force which individuals who act as representatives of the state may use. Physical force which goes beyond these limits is considered to be illegitimate or excessive. So perhaps when we are thinking of the state and its authority, whether this authority is conceived of in legal or moral terms, the contrast between force and violence turns out to be at most a distinction between violence and legitimate or non-excessive physical force.

Do we want to say that violence is always wrong, whereas physical force is only sometimes wrong and that, moreover, when wrongly applied it is violence, or at least a species of violence? In what follows I shall take this to be a question only about whether violence is always morally wrong. In discussions of violence, it has been suggested that etymology may be revealing. 'Violence' is a combination of two Latin words, *vis* and *latus*, 'force' and 'carried.' From this it would seem that the important thing about violence is that it is force plus something else, and this something else has to do with the way that force is carried out or applied. Violence violates necessarily, while force does not, at least not necessarily. But what does violence violate? Newton Garver writes, 'What is fundamental about violence in human affairs is that a person is violated. . . . If it rings true to talk about violating a person, that just is because a person has certain rights which are undeniably, indissolubly, connected with his being a person.' Garver goes on to say that, 'The right to one's body and the right to autonomy are undoubtedly the most fundamental rights of persons.'[2] But is it true, as Garver suggests, that violence in violating a person necessarily violates his rights?

What I question in comparisons of force and violence is the lesson these comparisons allegedly teach, namely that violence is always or necessarily a species of wrongdoing while force is not, or at least need not be, any such thing. More specifically I reject the claim that violence is always or necessarily a violation of someone's rights. Where acts of violence are concerned I am willing to acknowledge that such acts are aimed at inflicting harm or injury, while denying that all harms or injuries involve rights violations.[3] It might, however, be objected that since we have a natural duty not to harm or injure others,[4] and since duties and rights are correlative where the issue of harm or injury is concerned, isn't it the case that an act of violence is necessarily a violation of the right not to be harmed or injured? Before this question can be answered we need to examine briefly the question of what it is to have a right.

In the history of philosophical discussions of rights there was initially a tendency to regard at least some rights, the so-called natural rights (to life, liberty, and property, to give the more or less standard examples), as being absolute, but this led to the rejoinder that, since rights may sometimes conflict with one another, no right could be regarded as absolute in the sense of prevailing or obtaining under all circumstances. Thus, natural rights came to be construed as prima-facie rights, which meant that there was a strong presumption that a natural right would prevail unless there was an even stronger argument showing why it should not prevail in a given set of circumstances. But the objection to this was that now it would seem that the question of whether someone actually had a right might depend on the resolution of difficulties or disputes which might arise at some future time, and to some philosophers this seemed to undercut the whole concept of natural rights, which are said to be 'self-evident.' More recently, there has been an interesting attempt to show that there is at least one absolute natural right, which is that of all persons to be treated as persons; but even if there is such a right I find it difficult to determine how this discovery is going to affect our treatment of more traditional natural rights, such as the rights to life, liberty, and property. After all, the notion that natural rights should be interpreted as prima-facie rights came into being in large part as a way of handling cases where rights conflict, or appear to do so. Finally, in the contemporary discussion of rights we find the denial that rights *can* conflict, conflicts now being thought to occur only in the area of rival or competing claims to a right: on this analysis there could only be competing prima-facie claims to a right, and a right would obtain only in cases where a prima-facie claim was shown to be valid.

Instead of trying here to decide which of these ways of thinking about natural rights is ultimately the correct one, let us regard them simply as three possible descriptions of the alleged natural right not to be harmed or injured. And let us ask whether such a right could best be described as an absolute right, a prima-facie right, or a right which would only exist if a prima-facie claim to it were shown to be valid. Of the three possibilities I have mentioned, it seems most difficult to see how the right not to be harmed or injured could be said to be absolute. Traditionally we have tended to think that this right could under some circumstances be forfeited, annulled, or overridden. Even if we accept the newer reading of at least one natural right as being absolute, it does not follow from the one absolute natural right that has been argued for, namely the right of persons to be treated as persons, that a person has an absolute right not to be harmed; on the contrary, this allegedly absolute right has been used to defend the practice of punishment for wrongdoing along the lines of Hegel's famous 'right to be punished' – to deny someone such a right is now said to constitute a violation of his or her personhood. But, even if successful, this argument cannot show, nor was it meant to show, that punishment thereby ceases to be a harm to the person undergoing it; rather the claim is that not punishing someone may be a greater harm in the sense of constituting a denial of personhood.[5]

I want now to neglect chronology and turn to the most recent analysis of a right in terms of a valid claim. Here it would seem that the right not to be harmed or injured would have to be understood as involving initially a prima-facie claim to this right. A prima-facie claim is one which must be taken seriously, that is there must be good reasons to back it up, but of course not all good reasons turn out on inspection to be conclusive, and so not all prima-facie claims will turn out to be valid.[6] The right not to be harmed or injured failed to qualify as an absolute right because there were circumstances where it seemed appropriate to regard it as having been forfeited, annulled, or overridden, as, for example, in cases where an agent has himself inflicted unjustified harm or injury on others; and in these cases one might also expect such an agent's claim to the right not to be harmed or injured to turn out to be invalid. Given the logic of claims disputations, it seems possible that for some reason or other all prima-facie claims to the right not to be harmed or injured might fail to pass critical scrutiny. This is, of course, highly unlikely, but what is likely is that the prima-facie claim to the right not to be harmed or injured would fail in at least some cases, with the result that in those cases where an agent has inflicted unjustified harm or injury upon others violence directed against him might not constitute a violation of any of his actual rights. So if we want to say that violence is necessarily a rights violation, there seems to be just one possibility left open: violence should be regarded as a violation of the prima-facie right not to be harmed or injured.

One difference between the analysis of a right in terms of a prima-facie claim which can be shown to be valid and the analysis of at least natural rights in terms of prima-facie or presumptive rights is this: a prima-facie claim to a right must be argued for before it can be shown to be a valid claim, while a prima-facie right must be argued against before it can be shown not to be an actual right. Thus, an advocate of the position that violence is necessarily the violation of the prima-facie right not to be harmed or injured would maintain that there is a strong presumption against the use of violence that must be rebutted in each case before the prima-facie right in question can be said not to obtain in that particular instance. However, even if this is true, it seems unlikely that I would now be committed to the thesis that the *definition* of violence must include reference to the fact that violence is necessarily the violation of the prima-facie right not to be harmed or injured. But in any event, this would still be considerably less than we started out with in this discussion since a prima-facie rights violation might on investigation turn out not to be a violation of any actual right. Also, it is noteworthy that once we start to distinguish acts of violence which do involve actual rights violations from those which do not, we begin to parallel our earlier discussion of force. Force may be moral or immoral, appropriate or excessive, and, if I am correct, there is no good reason why the same cannot be said of violence.

What about the claim that besides physical violence there can be psychological violence and even institutional violence? Since psychological violence, if there can be such a thing, might be perpetrated either by individuals or by institutions, a consideration of psychological violence should perhaps await our decision as to whether there can be institutional violence. It may be helpful to commence by distinguishing between 'violence' and 'acts of violence.' Perhaps part of the reluctance to acknowledge the possibility of non-physical violence comes from the failure to notice that, although 'acts of violence,' as this concept is ordinarily used, refers exclusively to physical violence, 'violence' is not so restricted. After all, Sophocles in *Antigone* speaks of Creon's violence against the gods;[7] and, although the concepts 'psychological violence' and 'institutional violence' are technical terms introduced by political activists or philosophers sympathetic to the cause of drastic political or social change, they may nevertheless prove to be illuminating.

Besides acts of violence, there are violent thoughts and violent people, and perhaps there are violent institutions as well. Violent thoughts typically reflect desires, wishes, or fantasies about doing physical harm or injury to others; violent people are those who, given appropriate circumstances, would do physical harm or injury to others; and so-called violent institutions do harm, if not actual physical harm or injury, to persons, perhaps by stunting or repressing their moral, intellectual, or social development. Physical violence may, of course, occur in the absence of violent thoughts, as in cases of sudden, more or less spontaneous outpourings of anger; and people who are not in any broad dispositional sense violent may engage in acts of violence, as in protecting themselves against aggressors; but when we speak of violent thoughts or violent people it is typically thoughts of or dispositions towards physical violence that we have in mind. However, when we speak of violent institutions and the harm they cause or help to bring about we need not think of actual or even threatened physical violence, though perhaps usually there is some such threat, open or veiled. Even the physical harms or injuries which such institutions may cause or at least contribute to may be the result not of physical violence but of other things; for example, the absence of adequate safeguards in the work place might simply reflect callous indifference on the part of the ruling class.

But, strictly speaking, are there actually violent institutions? The importance of this question is, I believe, largely dependent upon how the issue of holism versus methodological individualism is resolved. As a methodological individualist, I can think of an institution only in terms of activities by individuals done in accordance with the rules, norms and standards of that institution. Violent institutions, on this analysis, would involve individuals who act in concert in such a way as to bring about harmful results to other individuals. Sometimes these harmful results may be intentional, at other times they may be the unintended consequences of intentional behaviour. So long as violent institutions are conceived of in a fashion consistent with the tenets of methodological individualism, I have no quarrel with the claim that there are or may be violent institutions. Slavery, segregation, or rigidly enforced class distinctions may reasonably be said to be violent institutions; and the question of whether an institution is violent or 'merely' repressive or 'only' discriminatory may turn out to be mainly one of degree, depending upon how much harm is done by the institution in question or how the harm is done.

If we grant that there may be different kinds of violence, and that the violence done by institutions need not be limited to physical violence, then the question arises as to what is to count as a morally appropriate or justifiable response to the different kinds of violence done by violent institutions. In so far as the violence is physical, the answer seems reasonably straightforward. Physical violence whether perpetrated by isolated individuals or by individuals acting in concert as members or supporters of an institution seems morally speaking all of a piece and should be dealt with accordingly, although exactly how individual members of an institution should be dealt with may depend, among other things, on their roles in upholding or defending a given institution. Methodological individualism, if it has any moral significance at all, would presumably support this conclusion. It would seem that non-physical violence does not in itself warrant the use of physical violence by way of response. However, non-physical violence may, if it is serious, prolonged, or systematic enough, provide such a warrant. The point here is simple: physical violence directed against physical violence does not, when there is no effective alternative available, require special justification, whereas something more needs to be said about non-physical violence before physical violence can be justified as an appropriate response. Another way of putting this is that physical violence matches up far more easily with physical violence than with non-physical violence. We need to know much more about a case of non-physical violence than simply the fact that it is a kind of violence before we can begin to consider whether physical violence is an appropriate response; however, in the case of physical violence this need not be so. Thus, even if all violence were necessarily a rights violation, non-physical institutional violence might not be a violation of a right of sufficient importance or gravity to warrant a physically violent response. Of course, in situations where slavery or segregation exists, for example, we rarely find piecemeal rights violations, but rather a system of rights violations; and it may be that while no single rights violation, taken by itself, is sufficient to warrant physical violence as a response, a cluster of such rights violations would look altogether different. And, of course, in the 'real world' we would normally not expect to find violent institutions in which the actual or threatened use of physical violence plays no part.

If there are violent institutions, and if these institutions can do harms to individuals which are not always or exclusively physical in nature, then it would seem that what they do to individuals will often be some kind of psychological harm which, provided it is severe enough, might aptly be called psychological violence. And if institutions can perpetrate psychological violence, then there is no reason why individuals cannot do so as well. Indeed, if methodological individualism is correct, the only way in which institutions can correctly be said to 'do' anything is through the actions of individuals who are members of, or support, the institution in question. One very important way of stunting the moral, intellectual or social development of individuals is to convince them that they lack the capacity or potential for such development; the damage that can be done to their self-confidence or self-esteem might, provided it is severe enough, properly be called psychological violence. Certainly individuals acting on their own can inflict this kind of damage upon other individuals, but here individuals acting on behalf of institutions would seem to have certain significant advantages. Although one individual can surely inflict severe psychological harm upon another or other individuals, institutions have, as it were, a longer reach, can intimidate and harm more individuals in a more thoroughgoing way than single individuals operating 'on their own' can usually manage to do. The difference is fairly obvious. If, for example, you in your individual capacity say to a member of a racial minority that members of his race don't fare very well in graduate school, he may perhaps be harmed severely and even irreparably; still one can hope that he will not be, that he will shrug off what you have said as 'one man's opinion' or as irrelevant to his own prospects for success. If, however, acting as your department's graduate adviser, you say the same thing to him, the harmful effect will surely be magnified because now, in a sense, you may be presumed to have the institution 'to back you up.' Hence there is a big difference between what might be called 'personal' and 'official' discouragement.

If institutions can do psychological harm in a more systematic way than even the most resourceful isolated individuals can usually accomplish, individuals have one apparent advantage over institutions. Although institutions can cast a wider net, individuals can cast a finer one. Individuals acting on their own can disparage, ridicule, ignore, condescend toward, malign, libel, slander, and defame other individuals, can 'get under their skin' in a great variety of ways, some of which may go far beyond any explicit or implicit institutional mandate. Where psychological harm to individuals is concerned it may be appropriate to consider this a species of violence, whether the violence is institutional in origin or comes simply from individuals acting on their own initiative. However, and this is a pragmatic point about the use and effectiveness of language, the word 'violence' derives much of its force from being reserved for fairly serious occasions, and there is a risk of trivialization whenever a word becomes overly popular. The paradigm of violence continues to be physical violence, perhaps because the harm it does is often severe and more readily apparent. When we are tempted to speak, as sometimes we should, of psychological violence, we ought to consider, first, the severity of the harm involved and, second, the appropriateness of other, more traditional descriptions of what has transpired. For example, when feelings are hurt, there may be, as Gandhi believed, 'a subtle violence' involved. But sometimes, depending upon commonsense considerations such as whether the feelings were hurt intentionally, and how badly, it may be overblown or exaggerated to insist that even subtle violence was involved. Hurt feelings should perhaps sometimes be left simply as hurt feelings.

I have one additional point to make about physical violence. Perhaps someone might want to distinguish between violent activities and acts of violence. Someone might want to say of boxing or football, for example, that these are violent activities, but might hesitate to describe a punch thrown in a boxing match or a tackle made in a football game as an act of violence. 'Acts of violence,' someone might say, should refer only to acts that involve harms or injuries which are in no way consented to, or allowed, under the rules of some game. Someone might further maintain that what counts as an act of violence is not to be determined solely on behavioral evidence but is 'context dependent.' Indeed, we might not be able to determine whether something is actually an act of violence until we have answered the question of whether someone's rights have been violated. While I am sympathetic to much of the above, I would resist the suggestion that whether something is to count as an act of violence depends upon whether a rights violation has occurred. Obviously we don't want to say that a rights violation is a sufficient condition for something to count as an act of violence, else we would expect to find an act of violence whenever a rights violation occurs. Nor, as I have argued, should we consider an act of violence as necessarily involving the violation of any actual right.

The relevance of the above discussion of violence and force to the issue of terrorism is fairly clear: there is, as radicals never tire of telling us, already a great deal of violence in our world, and thus it is somewhat hypocritical to dismiss terrorism solely on the ground that it involves violence. Oreste Scalzone, a former professor of politics and philosophy at the University of Padua and a convicted terrorist, has said,

> One cannot pretend to forget first of all that violence exists, everywhere in the world, enormous systematic violence. . . . The question of violence is always ruled by concepts of *realpolitik*, this, when it is a matter of violence exercised by agents of state or by various groups sustained by one state or another. . . . The ethical problem of violence is only posed when the violence is exercised in one way or another by people without power.[8]

By 'systematic' violence, Scalzone means not the 'hidden violence' of exploitation, domination, and oppression which is 'crystallized in all our society, in all our wealth, in all our assets,' but the 'obvious violence' of killing people 'everywhere in broad daylight.' This systematic violence, though obvious, attracts little or no attention, on my interpretation of what Scalzone is saying, because it is exercised (for the most part quite openly) by agents of the state. Stripped of its radical ideology, Scalzone's commentary can be read as a reminder that we live in a world in which there are lots of coercive institutions, especially the state which claims an exclusive monopoly within its jurisdiction on the use of physical violence (or force). As a radical, Scalzone would undoubtedly insist that the systematic, obvious violence that is involved in the state's use of its police powers is a political expression of the hidden violence involved in economic exploitation, and that the obvious violence is there to protect the wealth and other assets of the ruling class. But once again, if we strip aside the ideology, Scalzone has made a sound point, namely that we should explore the *ground* for the state's claim to an exclusive monopoly on the use of physical violence, and that we should not rely on *realpolitik* considerations. In other words, the state's monopoly cannot be justified simply because it exists but only by a demonstration that it is morally legitimate. And in cases such as terrorism where there is a challenge to the moral legitimacy of this monopoly, we have two sets of conflicting claims that must be examined judiciously. It is not even enough to say that the state's monopoly on physical violence is justified because of the consent of the governed, since even in a majoritarian democracy the rights of minorities may be ignored or trampled upon; and majoritarian democracies which respect the rights of their minorities may not be so considerate where the rights of other states and their citizens are concerned.

If I am correct in my analytic point that violence does not necessarily involve a violation of an actual right, then it is not decisive either for a radical such as Scalzone to point out that the state in using its police powers is far more violent than the terrorist or for a conservative to condemn terrorism simply because it is violent. Where the violation of an actual right or rights occurs, whether as the result of violence by the state or by the terrorist, this is, of course, a grave matter. This is especially true if the rights violation involves violence against persons who in the liberal tradition are defined, in

Joel Feinberg's words, as rights bearers. Ideally, of course, we should condemn all rights violations and press for their correction, but as a practical matter of living in the world we may have to decide which rights violations are the most serious and demanding of immediate attention. The problem becomes even more complex when we realize that often, though not always, rights violations whether by the state or the terrorist occur in the very process of defending what the state or the terrorist perceives, correctly or not, as the rights of their constituents. In weighing the rights of those who are protected by the state's monopoly on force and those who are in various ways oppressed by the exercise of this monopoly, we need to do (at least) two things. First, we should keep in mind the fact that the rival or competing rights, or claims to rights, may not always be of the same magnitude. Thus, for example, my right to travel, while important, may not be as fundamental as your right to a national homeland. Second, and this is not an analytic point at all but a normative proposal, we should acknowledge the presumption that, where possible, the rights of the weak should take precedence over the rights of the strong.[9] I think the intuition behind this recommendation concerns justice as fairness. It is often said, correctly I believe, that we in the liberal democracies have so many of the benefits that society can confer, while Third World countries have so few, that it behooves us to assist them even at some real inconvenience to ourselves. If we transpose this point about benefits to the treatment of rights, or claims to rights, it may be that the curtailment of some of our rights as a way of dealing more fairly or equitably with the rights of less fortunate nations or individuals can be warranted in the name of justice, and could perhaps even be shown to be in accord with the provisions of certain theories of justice such as Rawls' theory which argues that attention must be given both to providing equal opportunities for all and to alleviating the needs of the 'representative worst off man' (or nation).[10]

4 Innocence, just wars, and terrorism

Perhaps the main obstacle to any agreement that terrorism may in some circumstances be morally justifiable lies in the claim that it involves the violation of the rights of innocent persons. No matter what can be said about terrorism in self-defense or as a possible way of contributing to various desirable consequences, or about the moral legitimacy of violence under certain circumstances, it is terrorism's violation of the alleged rights of the allegedly innocent that seems to matter the most, and perhaps rightly so. Accordingly, in this chapter I shall consider certain questions about innocence, questions which I at least have found to be unexpectedly perplexing. What after all is an innocent person?

Is an innocent person one who has done no wrong, in which case only babies and very young children would seem to qualify? Or is an innocent person one who poses no threat of harm? Again, babies and very young children seem to qualify, but what about non-combatants in time of war? According to the just war tradition, non-combatants do seem to qualify: either they have the right to be left alone, unharmed, by warring parties, or, as a matter of chivalry, they ought to be unmolested. In the medieval period when war was largely the preserve of the knightly class, the distinction between combatants who did pose a threat of harm and non-combatants who did not was fairly easy to make, but in the modern period warfare has become more democratic, and the 'poor simple folk' who were to be exempt, on whatever grounds, from its harsher consequences figure more prominently in the 'war effort.' Many of them have now become combatants, while others contribute by their products or services to sustaining the war. Are non-combatants innocent only if they do not contribute directly to the war effort? Are non-combatants who contribute to the war effort by manufacturing weapons deprived of their innocence, while non-combatants who only grow food for the military still hold on to theirs? What about a farmer who grows a high-protein crop which will be used exclusively by the military? Is the distinction between support for the military as military and support for the military as human beings a morally significant one? Traditionally doctors and other medical personnel have been accorded non-combatant status even when they have been engaged in the care and treatment of combatants, but is a doctor treating a soldier who will return to combat on a par with one treating a soldier who will be returned to civilian life, or with one who treats civilians only? In a war of 'total mobilization' is everyone so involved that none can truly be called an 'innocent civilian'? In such circumstances is there anyone who poses no threat of harm?

George Habbash, leader of the Popular Front for the Liberation of Palestine, has claimed that in today's world no one is innocent. While this claim appears overstated, it serves to call attention to the ways in which societies and wars between them in the modern period differ from anything that existed previously. Perhaps Habbash can be read as saying that there was a time when some people were, or could have been, innocent. In another context, Lenin remarked that everything is related to everything else, and if we transpose this remark to the problem that concerned Habbash we may end up with something like this: at least in today's world everything is related to everything else in such a way that no one is innocent. Who in this interconnected world of ours poses no threat of harm? Suppose harm is taken to include both indirect and potential harm. Surely many non-combatants, including those who only support the military as human beings, pose at least the threat of indirect harm, and even when a war is in progress many, perhaps most, combatants pose at any given time only a potential harm to the enemy. How else to describe a soldier just beginning his training or playing a game of softball thousands of miles from the front? But if we expand the notion of harm to include potential harm, might not even babies and young children begin to appear threatening? In olden (more barbaric?) times the enemy reportedly slew his adversaries' families on the ground that if he did not the children would be raised by their mothers to avenge the death of their fathers. So the problem becomes one of how to contain or limit the notion of harm so that Habbash's claim continues to appear overstated.

Then there is the problem of innocence in the sense of ignorance and, relatedly, of inexperience. We love the innocence of children, but innocence in adults may seem less attractive, may indeed be seen as posing a risk or threat to their own interests. In the case of statesmen, for example, innocence of the true intentions of their nation's rivals may pose a threat to the very survival of that nation. 'Ignorance is bliss' can be a heavy bit of irony, carrying the unspoken message 'so long as it lasts,' and perhaps the same is true of innocence conceived of as a kind of ignorance. And, of course, the term 'innocents abroad' is rich with the suggestion of impending perils, which may be as good a way as any of bringing our attention to the problem of the hypothetical American tourist who proclaims, with an air of injured innocence, 'But what have I done?' In fact he just arrived last night, and, armed only with his American Express card, he could scarcely seem to pose a threat of harm to anyone. Perhaps, though this is increasingly difficult to imagine, he is innocent in the sense of being ignorant of the fact that he is perceived, rightly or wrongly, as a member of an enemy or hostile nation by many groups and movements around the world. That it is often difficult to imagine how anyone could be as innocent as he claims calls attention to an intriguing aspect of the problem. Much as some people cling desperately to their youth, so others hold on to their innocence. Here perhaps we begin to encounter willful ignorance, or willful innocence; and complicity in wrongdoing, which can take so many insidious forms, may arise from a self-deception which refuses to acknowledge the evil in the world or in oneself. In this context Habbash's claim that in today's world no one is (truly) innocent may be read as a thesis about the threat of harm which may be posed by an entire nation or group; more specifically, it can perhaps be read as a denial that one's ignorance of the wrongs allegedly done by one's nation or group is an excuse providing an exemption from punishment or retaliation for the 'wrongs' in question. Of course, it would be fallacious to infer that because a nation or group poses a threat of harm every individual member of that nation or group poses such a threat, but if harm is taken to include not only direct but indirect and potential harm then it becomes increasingly difficult to determine which individuals pose no threat of harm. Moreover, to the extent that a nation or group is democratic, then participation in policy-making procedures, even by something sometimes as remote as simply voting in a general election, or not using one's opportunity to vote, may widen considerably the net of responsibility, and in a democratic society with a free press and mass education per-haps it becomes truly the case that 'ignorance is no excuse.' Of course, the notion of posing a threat of harm is essentially prospective; and what George Habbash may have had in mind in denying that anyone is innocent was some idea about collective guilt, about the ways in which members of a community share in responsibility for wrongs which have previously been committed by that community; in this respect the denial of innocence is essentially retrospective.

This brings us to what may be a fourth sense of 'innocence,' one which involves a throwback or partial return to our first sense of 'innocence' and which is probably uppermost in the minds of those familiar with the criminal law. This is 'inno-cence' not in the sense of having done no wrong, which has a theological or at least a metaphysical ring to it, but in the sense of not having done the specific or particular wrong with which one has been charged. Georges Ibrahim Abdallah, the founder of the Lebanese Revolutionary Armed Faction, said in his trial in France in July, 1986, 'I am not a criminal. I am a combatant.' This may seem at odds with Habbash's claim that in today's world no one is innocent, the force of which is surely in the direction of collapsing the distinction between combatants and non-combatants. But Abdallah appears to be falling back upon this distinction, at least to the extent of claiming that he should be found innocent of the criminal charges brought against him because of his special status as a combatant. (Here it might be noted that, whether Abdallah knew it or not, the just war tradition has essentially two things to say about captured combatants: first, criminal charges should ordinarily not be brought against them; second, since they no longer pose a threat of harm, they should be treated as humanely as possible.) The court was unimpressed by Abdallah's claim, which, however, poses some interesting problems for the student of terrorism. If terrorists are combatants, should their attacks upon the enemy be limited to other combatants, and do they forfeit their status as combatants if they commence to attack non-combatants? And if terrorists aspire to become combatants, how do they do so? There are various, rule-governed ways in which individuals join military forces the world over, but what is to stop someone from setting up shop on his own, as it were, and proclaiming, 'Henceforth I am to be considered a combatant'? Perhaps one might refuse to become exercised by this problem and say I don't care what you call them, terrorists simply are people who behave in a certain manner. But criminals might behave in the same way (where overt physical actions are concerned), and no matter how terrifying criminals might be or become, some of us would resist a linguistic indifference which might appear to obscure fundamental and very real differences between, for example, the Mafia and the PLO. Nevertheless, some of us do insist that terrorists are criminals;

former President Reagan, for example, invariably referred to terrorists as 'cowards' and 'criminals.'

Any allegation of cowardice when applied to all terrorists is in one respect absurd: those who engage in suicide bombing missions and run the risk of highly probable death are hardly cowardly. They may, however, turn out to be cowards. If we distinguish between public and private violence, with public violence being carried on only by representatives of some legitimately constituted authority, then tradition (the Hague Conventions, for example) specifies that 'irregular' troops, troops operating behind enemy lines, must wear badges, have a recognizable leader, carry their arms openly, and abide by the rules of warfare. In the eyes of this tradition, terrorists could only appear as highly irregular: whenever possible they merge into the civilian, non-combatant population as a way of carrying out their campaign of violence, and rarely if ever do they carry their arms openly. There is a certain opprobrium attached to 'sneak attacks' even when carried out by regular combatants, and the more irregular the forces the greater this opprobrium becomes. Terrorists in particular might seem to be engaged in private violence, under cloak of civilian status, under cloak of darkness. Hence they might be branded cowards and criminals as well, since only public violence is recognized as legitimate violence. Here, in keeping with the just war tradition, we need to distinguish the question of whether a war is justifiable (*jus ad bellum*) from the question of how a war may be properly conducted (*jus in bello*). While *jus in bello* places many constraints upon how a war may be conducted, the one that is relevant here is that war must be fought only by representatives of legitimately constituted authority, must be public violence. Ultimately it would seem that whether terrorists can successfully be charged with being cowards and criminals depends upon whether they are subject to the same *jus in bello* constraints as irregular or guerrilla forces; this, of course, depends upon whether terrorists are rightly regarded as being in a state of war. If they are, then their methods of fighting violate some if not all the requirements of *jus in bello*, and their violence becomes private and criminal.

Certainly many terrorists would seem to regard themselves as being in a state of war (hence Abdallah's claim that he is a combatant), and terrorism is sometimes defined as 'war on the cheap.' Given the various kinds of war we have, limited or all-out war, declared or undeclared war, for example, it may well be that some terrorist activities should be regarded as war or part of a war. However, it seems doubtful that this can be true of all terrorist activities. Lenin said that the point or purpose of terrorism is to terrorize, and although this is not a complete characterization of terrorism, it is in no way an accurate characterization of war. What Lenin left out, among other things, is the way in which terrorism seeks to call attention to the alleged justice of its cause, and publicity for one's cause is not, typically, a reason why wars are fought. War is aimed at the defeat of an alien, external, or foreign power, and revolution is aimed at the overthrow or removal of some government;[1] and while terrorism may share either or both of these goals the important thing here is that it need share neither of them. Typically, terrorism may seek to coerce or frighten a government or a people into making changes which the terrorist believes cannot be brought about, or brought about as effectively, by other means; also, typically, terrorism may seek to publicize a grievance and thus gain support for its cause in the eyes of local or world opinion. Terrorism conceived of as a *strategy* may be part of a war or a revolution but that is not to say that it is always or necessarily part of a war or revolution.

Then there is the problem of legitimacy which seems so central to the just war tradition: do the combatants represent some clearly recognizable authority or government? This question, if it matters at all where terrorism is concerned, lies more on the periphery. It might, for example, be enough for a terrorist movement simply to claim to represent the aspirations or the moral rights of a people, or a group within a country, without much, if any, attention being paid to the question of how, by what legal or quasi-legal steps, it came to represent these aspirations or rights. Here moral authority may be all that matters. Governments, of course, need to be legitimated, which is one reason why governments in exile and movements like de Gaulle's Free French 'government' often have so problematic a status in the eyes of other governments; and, if and when the time for negotiations arrives, terrorist groups may encounter similar difficulties. It might be possible, for example, for someone to recognize the PLO's moral authority or right to speak or act on behalf of the Palestinian people while balking at the idea that this organization should be its legal or sole legal representative at the bargaining table once negotiations for the establishment of a Palestinian homeland are allowed to commence. But I find it difficult to see how the question of legitimacy could have the same moral significance for terrorism that it has for the standing of regular or irregular combatants in time of war.[2] In a way one could picture Abdallah (and Reagan) as being imprisoned, conceptually speaking, in a tradition where, once one engages in violence, one must be considered either a combatant or a criminal. Once we cease, however, to picture terrorists as being necessarily irregulars or guerrillas, the possibilities become more numerous. Of course, one might still find all terrorists to be criminals, but if so it is doubtful whether a single reason will explain why this judgment applies to all terrorists. If it is true that not all terrorists are engaged in war, then those who are not engaged cannot be pronounced criminals by virtue of any violation of the rules of war. If those terrorists who are not engaged in war are found to be criminals it will have to be for a different reason or reasons, and it may turn out that for at least some terrorists the charge of criminality cannot be made to stick at all.

It is, however, a mark of the continued relevance of the just war tradition that, even if we conclude that terrorism differs significantly from war, some aspects of the just war doctrine may remain useful in our moral assessment of terrorism.[3] In particular the distinction between the justification for undertaking a war and constraints upon how a war may be fought can be transposed to the discussion of terrorism. However shaky the distinction between combatant and non-combatant has become in the modern age and however perplexing we may find the notion of innocence, we are not, I hope, in a position where either indiscriminate warfare or indiscriminate terrorism becomes warranted. Here a significant resemblance between war and terrorism needs to be noted: like war, terrorism can be as selective or as indiscriminate as we wish to make it without thereby ceasing to be the kind of activity it is. If ours is an age marked by the loss of innocence, it does not follow that this applies equally over entire communities (as Habbash may have wished to suggest), or that we cannot distinguish, for example, between different kinds and degrees of complicity in wrongdoing, and conduct our struggles accordingly.

Part 2

Collective responsibility

5 Responsibility for the My Lai Massacre

On March 16, 1968, the soldiers of Charlie Company, 1st Battalion, 20th Infantry Division, of the United States Army, rounded up and killed as many as 500 unarmed women, children, and elderly Vietnamese in the hamlet of My Lai 4 in Son My, South Vietnam. Charlie Company had entered My Lai 4 expecting to encounter Viet Cong, but when they did not, they proceeded to slaughter its civilian occupants. Lt. William L. Calley gave the orders to kill these civilians, and he himself was subsequently charged with and convicted of some of the murders.[1] The My Lai Massacre, when it was revealed, led to a 'crisis of conscience' in the American people. According to some commentators, it resulted in a 'loss of innocence' among many who had apparently believed that their compatriots would never behave as Lt. Calley and some (but not all) of his troops had. Some people believed that Lt. Calley was innocent of the charges brought against him or that he himself was 'only following orders.' Others saw him as a 'scapegoat,' not perhaps in the sense that he was innocent but that he had been unfairly singled out for punishment for doing what other soldiers had done in wartime. Some professed to believe that the My Lai Massacre, while regrettable, did not reflect badly upon America, and that Lt. Calley and only Lt. Calley was responsible for what he had done, while others blamed the men of Charlie Company for not trying to stop him. Many people, however, had the uneasy feeling that while Lt. Calley's conduct was reprehensible and deserving of punishment, the ultimate responsibility for what he had done rested with 'the system,' though it was not always clear what system they had in mind.

Philosophers who have commented on the My Lai Massacre have tended to reflect and to elaborate upon some, but not all, of these sentiments. In my judgment perhaps the most ambitious and provocative work done by a philosopher in this connection has been David Cooper's 'Responsibility and the "system,"' which is an extension of an earlier essay, 'Collective responsibility' (1968), devoted to the problem of collective but non-distributive responsibility.[2] I shall examine Cooper's two essays, in the order in which they were written, as a way of developing some of my own views on the responsibility for My Lai and on collective responsibility.

David Cooper's 'Collective responsibility' commences with an attack upon methodological individualism. He maintains that statements about collectives are not equivalent in meaning to statements about individuals:

> This is because the identity of a collective does not consist in the identity of its membership. The local tennis club is the same club as it was last year, despite the fact that new members may have joined, and old ones departed.[3]

Cooper is undoubtedly correct in maintaining that 'the existence of a collective is compatible with a varying membership,' but his claim that the tennis club is, or can be, the same tennis club even with changes in membership is controversial. Criteria for the identity of individuals are in dispute, so must we wait until this problem is resolved before we can hope to do justice to criteria for the identity of collectives, and will the criteria be all that different? Continuous memories are sometimes said to be essential for personal identity. The chancellor who embezzled the money is said not to be the 'same man' as the one who reformed the university, but this seems just a dramatic way of underscoring the suddenness or severity of his lapse; by contrast the amnesiac who used to be a chancellor but remembers nothing of this or any other aspect of his previous life can much more plausibly be said not to be the same man he once was. In collectives what would take the place of continuous memory as a criterion for identity? Minutes of meetings or memoirs by members? If Cooper is correct, and members who might have remembered the past or some part of the past history of the local tennis club may come and go without it ceasing to be the same club, then it may be difficult to determine what could take the place of memory as a criterion for identity. Perhaps an unchanging constitution with a fixed decision procedure might suffice, the idea here being that while club presidents, for example, might come and go the presidency itself would remain.

This is not a merely theoretical difficulty since Cooper goes on to claim that the statement, 'the local tennis club is responsible for its own closure,' is not to be treated as a propositional function of the form, 'if anyone is a member of the tennis club, then he is partly responsible for the closure of the club.' Perhaps a particular member or indeed all the members of the club might bear some or all the responsibility for its closure, but Cooper maintains that this need not be the case and that in fact no member of the club need be responsible for its closure. However, while Cooper is undoubtedly correct in saying that not every member of the club need be even partly responsible for its closure (here we think of a recently recruited member, or one who has been out of the country for years), the fact that members of a collective may come and go does not mean that we cannot insist upon holding some particular member or members of a given collective responsible for a specific act by that collective. In the tennis club example, on the level of causal responsibility, if the club is not closed by an external action such as a foreclosure or some other court action, then presumably some individual member(s) or officer(s) must have decided to close the club; and while these individuals may or may not be the ones who are morally responsible for the closure of the club, it is difficult to see in

Cooper's claim – that the identity of a club can persist over time despite membership changes – anything which would support the assertion that no particular member(s) need be responsible for the closure of the club. Of course, it may be the case that there need not be any *moral* responsibility for the closure of a tennis club, but in the event that there is such a responsibility, as Cooper assumes in his example, the methodological individualist could still insist that some individual agent(s) must be responsible.

There is, however, an interesting historical dimension to Cooper's tennis club example, which is sometimes absent in other examples of collective non-distributive responsibility such as Joel Feinberg's case of a group of train passengers who fail to resist a robbery by the Jesse James gang.[4] The closure of the tennis club as envisaged by Cooper is a rather long-drawn-out affair. There was a failure of *esprit de corps*, everyone tried to be friendly, but there was 'always a certain tension.' But was it always the same tension in the same club if there was a significant or even total change of membership? And was its closure necessarily a failure, moral or otherwise, if there was a total change of membership, and the new members came in not to enjoy the privileges of the club but, say, to close it and sell off its property? A tennis club may come into being for one purpose (tennis?), continue for another (one's parents belonged), and close for yet another (to liquidate the assets). Will it still be the same tennis club if all the members change and the original purpose or function of the club also changes drastically?

Let us imagine that in Cooper's tennis club there are three fairly distinct stages or periods: the founding, a middle period, and the folding. Let us call them Stage 1, Stage 2, and Stage 3, respectively. In Stage 1 a constitution is drawn up, membership is solicited, officers are elected, funding is obtained, and a property is purchased. But once underway as an organized collective, the club takes on a life of its own. In speaking in this manner, one need not succumb to any 'holism,' or imagine that the club is an entity that somehow

acts independently of its members. But it is a way of acknowl-
edging that the rules, formal and informal, of the club direct
and constrain the activities of its members. New officers and
members are limited by decisions taken in the past, and there
are fewer options than there were in the beginning. In Stage
2 things slowly, at first almost indiscernibly, begin to go down-
hill: the members don't feel at ease with one another, and
the club just isn't as much fun as other tennis clubs are, or
are believed to be. Still, there is an atmosphere of cheeriness
if not of cheer, and there is a widespread belief that things
will right themselves in the end, that the club will muddle
through to better days. Meanwhile there is no emergency,
and heroic actions of any sort would be inappropriate because
of a general feeling of complacency and stagnation. In Stage
3 the club begins to fold. Members are increasingly absent,
dues go unpaid, and mortgage payments can't be met. In this
stage members come to realize that drastic changes must
be made or the club will go under. Here the list of options increases dramatically: a new body of officers, or a
membership drive, or a fundraising gala, or refurbishing the
old property, or the purchase of a new facility in a better part
of town, and so on. Action is still inhibited by the decisions
of the Founding Fathers in Stage 1 and by the gradual deterio-
ration that characterized Stage 2, but now the club can attempt
things which would have been difficult or impossible in that
second period. Stage 3 resembles Stage 1 in that new begin-
nings are needed, and at least some individuals, especially
officers and influential members, can reasonably be expected
to make a considerable effort to keep the club from failing.

In Stage 1 certain individuals joined together to form a
tennis club. What we had here was no 'random collective' of
the sort discussed by Virginia Held,[5] and surely there was no
responsibility, individual or collective, to undertake to form a
tennis club. Nevertheless, once they did so, the Founding
Fathers could be held collectively as well as individually
responsible for what they did. Here each individual Founding Father would be responsible not only for his individual

contribution to the forming of the club but for the decisions and actions which the Founding Fathers took as a group. To be sure, particular individuals would be more or less responsible for what was done, depending among other things upon their influence on the other Founding Fathers, but it is difficult to imagine one who was in no way responsible for what they did as a group. (Even a 'token' Founding Father who did nothing but allow his name to be used would bear some real, non-token responsibility.) In Stage 2 there was a collective responsibility for the sub-standard performance of the club; but whether or not any individual members were sub-standard or at fault in their conduct, the club's performance would still have been sub-standard. In Stage 3, to use Karl Popper's suggestive phrase, 'the logic of the situation' was different, and there were new options. There was now a collective responsibility, but one with significant individual distributions, to face up to a new problem situation and try to overcome it. Reforms that would have been impractical or unacceptable in Stage 2 might in the crisis atmosphere of Stage 3 have seemed entirely reasonable and appropriate. If in fact some individuals were responsible for the, as it were, genteel malaise that began to affect the club in Stage 2, they could well be the actors who were involved in Stage 1: perhaps it was their mistakes or miscalculations which ultimately led to the club's being less than it should have been, and one can imagine that perhaps none of these actors was still active or even present during most or all of Stage 2. If, however, the malaise of Stage 2 were to go uncorrected in Stage 3, then the responsibility for this would be both collective and distributive over at least some of the members, with club officers and influential members perhaps bearing the brunt of that responsibility. One final note here: the three stages in the history of the club are distinct from one another in terms of their problem situations; and while I have spoken of these stages as involving membership changes in the club, the membership could have been constant over all three stages without affecting our ability to distinguish the three stages, and their attendant responsibilities, from one another.

Where does this leave the methodological individualist? Significantly better off, I think, than would a non-historical treatment of collective but non-distributive fault, since in my example we are able to say with some precision when the fault is and is not distributive. In my account of the tennis club there is a beginning and an ending in which particular individuals are clearly responsible for the performance of the club. In Stage 2 it is true that there may be no individuals who are responsible for the club's difficulties, but this is only because the logic of the situation limits the possibilities of effective reform. Even then, it is arguable that something might have been done in the way of modest piecemeal changes. Someone, it is arguable, should have noticed when the slide began and alerted others to the problem before it became acute. To say, as Cooper does, that his example of collective but non-distributive responsibility shows that ascriptions of moral responsibility can be made even when the collective in question could not have done otherwise, and to claim that this may be generalized to other cases of moral responsibility, involves a drastic overinterpretation of his own example. It may be difficult in many of the Stage 2s of this world to bring about change, to alert members of a collective to problems before they become acute. It is, however, arguable that in real-world situations it may often be no more difficult to make small corrections in Stage 2 than it is to make large corrections in Stage 3. Perhaps in some Stage 2s there are mitigating circumstances which help to excuse the failure of individuals to act, but surely this is not to say that individuals who find themselves in such situations and fail to attempt to rectify matters may be entirely faultless. Whatever our verdict about Stage 2 in my extended tennis club fable, it is clear that with the crisis of Stage 3 new options emerge, and individual responsibilities for the future, if any, of the tennis club can be more clearly delineated.

Even if we grant fully a Cooperian interpretation of my

Stage 2 there remains the question of how this would affect the collective liability of the tennis club. If I am correct, the answer is that legal liability (for what?) is out of the question and any moral liability would be extremely mild. A sigh of boredom, a warning to friends to avoid the dullness and stiffness of an afternoon or evening at the club, what more could there be in Stage 2? Of course, this might reflect unfairly upon members who are not dull or stiff, or who would not be in other contexts, but as liability goes this is about as gentle as ascriptions of liability get. By contrast liability in Stages 1 and 3 is a much graver affair. At Stages 1 and 3 we have the advantage that we can, given appropriate information, pick out specific individuals who deserve censure or blame for their contribution to the sub-standard performance of the collective to which they belong. It may be true, as Feinberg says, that ascriptions of collective liability necessarily fall upon all members of a collective, but there is no legal or moral reason why they need fall with equal weight upon all those members. In Stages 1 and 3 we can at least make distinctions in our ascriptions of liability which sometimes could not be made in Stage 2 if Cooper is correct. While any censure, however mild, of a collective *none* of whose members is at fault for its sub-standard performance might seem objectionable from the point of view of methodological individualism, if such censure must be made, then Stage 2 would be the place where morally speaking it would do the least harm.

I turn now to Cooper's essay 'Responsibility and the "system," ' in which he examines the problem of responsibility for the My Lai Massacre. Here instead of talking about a failed tennis club Cooper introduces a new example to illustrate his thesis about collective but non-distributive responsibility. Consider, he suggests, a small frontier township in the nine-teenth-century American west. For purposes of law and order the citizens form themselves into a vigilante committee which is not really interested in proper justice but only in protecting the interests of local citizens against those of strangers and citizens of other nearby townships. This practice continues for thirty years, and a 'typically unjust decision' is made against a wandering cowboy who is then driven out of town. A newspaperman in a neighbouring town writes that the vigilante committee of X-ville is responsible for the injustice against the cowboy in question.[6]

This condemnation of the committee may, according to Cooper, be justified. He maintains that we may condemn the committee, for it is due to its organization and practice that the cowboy received rough treatment; however, it is not clear, Cooper maintains, that any individual townsman in the committee can be condemned and blamed. Each member is simply following the practice which has become universal in the township, and if he tried to oppose the practice he and his family would risk ostracism or worse. Overall, Cooper's treatment of the vigilante committee parallels that of the tennis club, and I shall come back to it after I have outlined his analysis of the My Lai Massacre. However, three important differences should be kept in mind. First, it was, as noted earlier, by no means clear that the failure of the tennis club was necessarily a moral failure or one that reflected any moral deficiencies in any of its members. Second, even if the failure of the club to live up to standards set by other clubs could be described in moral terms, it was not a failure that caused any strangers who happened to come to the club any harm or injustice. Third, even if the club had been responsible for some harm or injustice done to a stranger, we have no reason to believe that this would reflect a common practice on the part of the club or of some committee representing it.

Cooper proceeds to consider whether non-distributive responsibility for atrocities in the Vietnam War can be ascribed to the US military system, this being taken to include not only American soldiers in Vietnam but also those who had some responsibility for training men and developing strategies for the war, and those who were in positions of authority for the conduct of the war. To condemn the system it must be shown that the men within it who committed the atrocities at My Lai were acting 'in accordance with sub-standard practices, rules or conventions governing that system's 'way of life' in Vietnam.'[7] Cooper then examines three possible explanations for the sub-standard practices, rules, or conventions in question.

Cooper considers and rejects Jean-Paul Sartre's charge that atrocities such as My Lai were genocidal crimes. There is no evidence, according to Cooper, that any of the Americans charged with committing an atrocity did so for the simple reason that his victims were Vietnamese; and none of those on trial for My Lai displayed any signs of racial hatred. As for the 'mere Gook rule,' Cooper denies that the existence or even prevalence of an informal 'rule' to the effect that the life of a Vietnamese is to be taken into little or no account would make a case against the military. The word 'Gook' alone tells us nothing since soldiers frequently apply unflattering epithets to both friend and foe, e.g. Kraut, Limey and Frog. Also, where soldiers are stationed among civilians, relations between the two groups are rarely good, and this difficulty may well have been compounded by the fact that the civilians in Vietnam were in looks, language and custom indistinguishable from the enemy. Still, according to Cooper, it is one thing to behave badly toward people because they belong to a different race, and quite another thing to behave badly toward people who happen to be of a different race but for reasons that may have nothing to do with race.[8]

Has Cooper succeeded in showing that racism is not a 'plausible candidate' for explaining the sub-standard characteristics of the American military system in Vietnam? One can readily grant Cooper that Americans in Vietnam may not have killed Vietnamese for the 'simple reason' that they were Vietnamese, and this is sufficient to refute Sartre's charge. Genocide, as ordinarily understood, involves a deliberate, systematic attempt to destroy another race or as many of its members as possible, and the absence of genocide does little if anything to establish the absence of racism. If no American ever killed a Vietnamese for the simple reason that he was Vietnamese, it seems plausible to suggest that the fact that he was Vietnamese may have made it a great deal easier to kill him. Martin Luther King claimed that we would not have dropped the atom bomb on Hiroshima or Nagasaki if the Japanese had belonged to the white race, and while this kind of claim involves a complex of counter-factuals it has a certain force. King, of course, was not saying that we dropped the atom bomb for the simple or sole reason that the Japanese were members of another race, nor was he saying that under no circumstances would we ever have dropped it on the Germans. What I think he was saying is that only in cases of absolute military necessity would we have dropped the atom bomb on the Germans, and that such circumstances did not obtain in the bombing of Hiroshima and Nagasaki. President Truman claimed that he gave the order to drop the bomb so as to save the lives of American troops that would have been lost had we invaded Japan; but it is disturbing that he claimed to have had no moral qualms about giving such an order and to have slept soundly the night after he did so. Moreover, Japan was already largely defeated, and perhaps an invasion might not have proved necessary. Perhaps a demonstration of the powers of the atom bomb on, say, a largely unpopulated island or two might have sufficed. As for the firebombing of Dresden and other largely civilian targets in Germany, this does not in my judgment support the claim that we would have used the atom bomb against the Germans to hasten the end of the war. Some evidence that seems to support the charge of racism against the military in Vietnam is that crimes by military personnel against the Vietnamese went largely unpunished by the military criminal justice system, in sharp contrast to the prompt and severe punishment meted out to American military personnel for crimes against Europeans in the Second World War. Either the military criminal justice system had grown unaccountably lax in two decades or there was a disposition to ignore or treat leniently crimes against the Vietnamese because they were members of another race. The 'mere Gook rule' is disturbing not because of its racial overtones but because of its substantive content: here we should note the absence of any 'mere Kraut rule' in the Second World War. Contrary to Cooper, I find that the existence of such a rule among military personnel makes a strong case against the military. By not moving to counteract or uproot it, the military command seems to have tacitly accepted the 'mere Gook rule.' As for the fact that none of those accused of the atrocities at My Lai displayed 'any signs of racist hatred,' it is well known that racism can be insidious and dispositional, and perhaps something less than all-out hatred would be sufficient to show that the soldiers in question were contemptuous of the lives of the Vietnamese at My Lai. It is, in any event, the attitude of the military *system* toward things such as the 'mere Gook rule' which is at issue. Since it was often difficult to distinguish friend from foe, an attitude of 'why bother?' seems to have been all too pervasive; it can plausibly be attributed at least in part to racism.

The second possible explanation for the sub-standard quality of the American military in Vietnam which Cooper considers and rejects is the training provided by the military system. Cooper rightly rejects the charge that Calley and his men were machine-like killers molded by irresistible training and indoctrination; he notes that the men in Charlie Company were raw, nervous recruits. What is more difficult to assess is the charge made by Lt. Calley, and supported by statements given by many other military personnel not involved in the My Lai Massacre, that the Army provided inadequate or non-existent instruction on the Geneva Convention dealing with the treatment of civilian populations and prisoners of war. If this charge is true, Cooper says, then the Army should be censured, but he thinks it is difficult to see how such inadequate instruction could have been responsible for My Lai: one does not require much instruction to know that one does not massacre unarmed civilians who are not prisoners anyway. As Judge Kennedy who presided over Calley's trial at Ft Benning, Georgia, put it, the issue is whether 'a man of ordinary sense and understanding' would see that it was unlawful to kill civilians as at My Lai. According to Cooper, 'to hold the army responsible on these grounds would be as absurd as holding the university authorities responsible for my setting fire to the classroom building on the grounds that they never told me I should not.'[9] But I find it absurd to compare Calley's situation to that of a university professor. It is, I think, true that a man of ordinary sense and understanding might well have behaved differently from Lt. Calley, as in fact most of his men did. This might help to establish not only the legal but the moral guilt of Lt. Calley, but it does not, as Cooper believes, settle the point at issue. While I have never heard of a university professor setting fire to a school building, the Army in Vietnam had evidence of numerous unwarranted killings of civilians by American soldiers long before the My Lai Massacre, and whatever may have been taught Calley and others in officers training school back in the States, the military had the responsibility for additional training and indoctrination once the officers and their men were in Vietnam. While the official policy may have been to win the hearts and minds of the Vietnamese, the more prevalent attitude in actual practice seems to have been that expressed by an officer quoted as saying that once you have them by their balls their hearts and minds will follow. Since it was often difficult to tell friend from foe, the Army was responsible for not having provided instruction as to what to do when in doubt. Again, as in the case of racism, the Army seems to have been negligent in not taking steps to prevent the unlawful killing of Vietnamese. It seems wrongheaded of Cooper to acknowledge that the Army deserves censure for inadequate instruction in the Geneva Conventions but to deny that this inadequate instruction could have contributed causally to the My Lai Massacre.

The third alleged characteristic of the system Cooper discusses, and the one he chooses to explain why the system was sub-standard, is the conduct of the war by the military system. He quotes Telford Taylor as saying that the ultimate question in the My Lai trial is how far these troops departed from the general military *practice* in Vietnam as they had witnessed it.[10] Taylor suggests that the departure was not very

great, and Cooper and I agree. Cooper cites free fire zones,
the emphasis on high body counts, the bombing of villages
of minimal military importance, the use of Vietnamese as
human mine sweepers, the deportation of civilians into appalling concentration camps, and the use of weapons such as
napalm; and he claims, I believe correctly, that these practices
were criminal and immoral. They were not indispensable for
the conduct of the war in Cooper's judgment, and I concur.
I will not repeat the many points Cooper and I agree on; my
complaint is that Cooper does not go far enough. First, as I
have indicated, there is no good reason not to include a
tolerance of racist attitudes and a failure to educate the troops
in the proper treatment of the Vietnamese among the sub-
standard practices of the military system. Second, the question
of how the war was conducted raises policy issues at the
highest political level, outside the control of the military
system. Noble pronouncements from Presidents Johnson and
Nixon about the effort to stop communism in Southeast Asia
and to win the loyalty of the South Vietnamese went hand in
hand with their acceptance of practices such as the use of
free fire zones and napalm bombs which were virtually guaran-
teed to cause us to lose not only the hearts and minds of the
South Vietnamese but of civilized people the world over; and
in fact we found ourselves more and more isolated from our
European allies as the war progressed. This had not happened
in the Korean War, so there was presumably something
especially repugnant about our conduct in Vietnam. Even if
the criteria for a just war (jus in bellum) were satisfied in
Vietnam, the criteria for a morally acceptable conduct of a
war (jus in bello) were plainly not. In fairness to the military,
while our government allowed the most heinous practices to
develop in the conduct of the war, especially in our treatment
of the people whose country we sought to defend, political
restrictions on how the war was to be carried into North
Vietnam, e.g. in the selection of bombing targets, although
understandable in terms of the fear of Russian or Chinese
entry into the war, made the task of the military extremely

difficult. Frustration at a 'no win' policy conjoined with the long duration of the war helped to create in the military a kind of 'displacement behavior': what could not be vented upon the enemy in North Vietnam could be vented upon any Vietnamese of questionable loyalty in South Vietnam. This is not to condone what Lt. Calley did, but the My Lai Massacre did not happen in a vacuum, and I fully approve Cooper's efforts to put it in the context of a system, though the one I have in mind is not limited largely or even mainly to the military system. I find myself, if anything, going beyond Cooper in finding the military (and political) system sub-standard in its conduct of the war in Vietnam, but I have doubts about some of the conclusions Cooper draws from the Vietnam experience where the question of collective responsibility is concerned. What is crucial here is what we think a system is and how we think a system operates.

Central to Cooper's analysis of a system is the idea of a practice. Cooper writes that after we have blamed specific individuals from generals (and presidents) on down to Lt. Calley and the men of Charlie Company, blame has not been exhausted. He would, apparently, blame 'the system' for allowing certain practices to obtain:

> *Practice* is made, or at least continued, by the myriad decisions of generals, colonels, majors, captains, lieutenants, or sergeants in the field or in the air. Soldiers come into Vietnam faced by a ready-made situation, with various policies and practices established as the norms. They proceed to act in accordance with these norms, hence perpetuating the system characterized by these norms. It seems that we do have a genuine *system* here; an organization in which men do not choose and act as isolated individuals, but as men having roles to play, rules to follow, and a way of life in which they are constrained. The position is surely similar to, on a larger scale, our vigilante system.[11]

Initially it would seem that there is nothing here which a

methodological individualist need contest, so long as the sub-standard conduct of the system is blamed upon decisions made by individuals throughout the military (and political) hierarchy. The 'way of life' and the rules, explicit and implicit, which constituted the American military organization in Vietnam and which constrained the actions of individuals in that organization were presumably determined at least in part by such decisions. Cooper concludes that

> the Calleys of the war are no doubt morally and criminally responsible. But a system which has developed its own momentum − and which is not the creature of a few individuals, but rather whose creatures most individuals are − must bear its share of responsibility for the 'unlovely circumstances' of the war, those circumstances which partially explain the existence of the Calleys.[12]

The methodological individualist could accept the claim that the system in question was not the creature of a few individuals, but he could also emphasize that, whether the system was the product of a few or many individuals, the actions of individuals frequently have unintended consequences which in turn affect future decisions and actions by these or other individuals. To deny, as Cooper does, that individuals are 'isolated' and to affirm that individuals (all of us) are the 'creatures' of some system(s) need not pose any special difficulties for the methodological individualist. All of us, he might say, are the creatures of circumstances if this is understood in terms of how these circumstances affect an individual's assessment of the 'logic' of the situation in which he finds himself. But, and here perhaps is a substantive disagreement, the methodological individualist would insist that it is an individual's assessment of the logic of the situation in which he finds himself, his own determination of the options which are open to him, not the circumstances themselves, which are in the final analysis decisive.

However the issues raised by collectivism versus methodological individualism may be resolved, Cooper is surely mistaken in maintaining that the position of the military in Vietnam is significantly similar to his example of the vigilante committee in X-ville, though on a larger scale. To be sure, in both cases individual actions are in some sense constrained by the system of which the individuals are a part, but where the issue of collective responsibility is concerned significant differences emerge. Cooper, we may recall, makes two claims about the vigilante committee: (1) that we may condemn the committee for the unjust treatment accorded the cowboy; and (2) that it is not clear that any individual townsman in the committee can be condemned or blamed. What Cooper's analysis of My Lai really establishes is that the military system and some, but not all, of the members of that system were responsible, in varying ways, for the massacre. It is, therefore, wrong for Cooper to maintain that the military system in Vietnam was similar but on a larger scale to his vigilante committee example, for scale has nothing to do with the fact that responsibility could be distributed over some but not all of the members of the military system in Vietnam. Cooper maintained that the citizens of X-ville had simply been born into the vigilante way of doing things, but while this may have some plausibility in the case of a small isolated community, it has far less plausibility where the military system in Vietnam was concerned. No one was born into the military system in Vietnam though many, but not all, of the soldiers accepted its common practices once they arrived. If I may alter Cooper's example, the military system in Vietnam was more like a military outpost or garrison than an isolated town, and an outpost in constant communication with the larger military (and political) system of which it was a part. What happened in this outpost was often the direct result of commands, and pressures, from high-level generals and political leaders at home; for example, the efforts of Presidents Johnson and Nixon to secure support for the war from an increasingly divided Congress and citizenry led to pressures on our military leaders in Vietnam for high body counts; this in turn led to the falsification of figures sent to Washington and contributed indirectly to the indiscriminate slaughter of civilians in South Vietnam. Thus, even if a 'way of life' had emerged in Vietnam which made My Lai and other atrocities possible, the military system in Vietnam was not closed to anything like the extent that X-ville was in Cooper's vigilante example. Accordingly, responsibility for what happened in the military system in Vietnam rested in large part upon the military and political system of the United States.

The 'way of life' of the American military system in Vietnam to which Cooper attaches such importance was, if I am correct, an extension of the 'American way of life' in several respects. First, there was the racism of the American way of life which found exaggerated expression in phenomena such as the 'mere Gook rule.' Second, and this is far more complicated, the conduct of the leaders of our political system in their handling of the war must have had a corrupting influence upon the conduct of the leaders of our military system in Vietnam. Duplicity abounded on all levels. There was President Johnson with his Gulf of Tonkin Resolution which justified a widening American involvement in the war on the basis of a non-existent attack by North Vietnamese naval vessels, and President Nixon who won the election in 1968 in large part upon the basis of a 'secret' (non-existent) plan to end the war. Small wonder that General Westmoreland not only sent exaggerated numbers of enemies killed back to Washington but systematically downgraded the number of North Vietnamese supporters in South Vietnam.[13] Several witnesses quoted Westmoreland as asking what could he tell the President, the Congress and the press. Apparently telling the truth was not a live option, and there was the suspicion that he could tell President Johnson only what President Johnson wanted to hear.

What was the responsibility of American citizens for the war in Vietnam? In both the elections of 1964 and 1968 the majority could plausibly be said to have voted for a 'peace' candidate, first Johnson who promised to limit our involvement in the war, then Nixon who promised to end it as soon as possible; and the duplicity of Johnson, Nixon and Westmoreland went largely undetected until it was too late. There was, however, enough evidence of duplicity to help turn many of 'the brightest and the best' from architects and supporters of the war into its severest critics: never before had the 'intellectual elite' been so alienated from the 'system.' Still, the 'silent majority' supported our leaders even as evidence of duplicity mounted and it became clear that the war could not be won. In this, as in many wartime situations, there is a disquieting parallel between the citizen's claim that he is only supporting his leaders and the soldier's claim that he is only following orders. The fact that we are at war may limit our options significantly, whether we are mere civilians or soldiers in the field. And the fact that we were at war, an unusually prolonged and frustrating war, was undoubtedly the catalyst which was (causally) responsible for much that was morally despicable about the manner in which our system reacted to the war. The 'American way of life' in the 1960s reflected initially a great idealism and optimism on several fronts: domestically, there was the civil rights movement against segregation and the 'war' on poverty; and the war in Vietnam was perceived as a struggle against communism and aggression from North Vietnam. Ironically, however, the racism which received a severe set-back at home found a new, more hospitable setting in the field in Vietnam, and the 'war' against poverty was lost in the war against North Vietnam which in its turn was also lost. I remember hearing the ebullient Hubert Humphrey say that we could afford both guns and butter when actually we could afford neither. The 'American way of life' was severely fractured by the Vietnam War and was seen as operating under priorities and rules which frequently seemed incompatible with one another; and this in turn had to have an adverse effect upon our military system in Vietnam. If ever there was a vicious circle this was it; and indeed the whole situation seems far removed from Cooper's frontier township, with its stable, cohesive set of priorities and rules reflecting a unanimous consensus of opinions and values.

Where does this leave us regarding the issue of collective non-distributive responsibility? According to the position Cooper takes in his second essay, collective non-distributive responsibility can be related to individual responsibility in three possible ways: (1) there is the case where no individual member of the group need be held responsible; (2) there is the case where although certain individuals are held responsible to some degree the responsibility of the group is not exhausted by these individual responsibilities; and (3) there is the case where each individual member of the group is held individually responsible but where the responsibility of the group is something more than the sum of all these individual responsibilities. One might quarrel, as I do, with Cooper's decision to classify all three ways as involving collective non-distributive responsibility since in (2) and (3) some or all individual members of the collective are being held responsible; but where (2) and (3) are concerned what Cooper is saying is that even after a distribution of responsibility over some or all the individual members of a collective there will remain some responsibility which is not exhausted by these individual distributions and which attaches to the collective, not to any of its individual members. I believe that Cooper was mistaken in reaching the conclusion that the vigilante committee in X-ville is an example of (1) and that it can help illuminate the collective responsibility for the My Lai Massacre. By Cooper's own account the citizens of X-ville might be considered 'weak or convention-bound,' but he denies that any of them need be considered 'evil.' He does not consider the possibility that in some circumstances to be weak or convention-bound just is to be evil, or if this is contested, it is at least a way of allowing evil to occur. In any event, what Cooper actually says about the responsibilities of military officers in Vietnam ranging from high-ranking generals to Lt. Calley fits (2). (It does not fit (3) because many of Calley's men refused to obey his orders, and one pilot when he observed what was happening at My Lai landed his helicopter and heroically rescued some of the Vietnamese civilians from Lt. Calley at gunpoint.)

If the My Lai Massacre is properly interpreted as an example of collective responsibility distributed over some but not all the members of the collective, in this case the American military system in Vietnam, what are we to make of Cooper's claim that even after such a distribution the responsibility for My Lai is not exhausted and that the military system itself is somehow at fault? I think this claim invites some initial skepticism: how do we know responsibility is not exhausted until *after* all the individual distributions have actually been made? If we say that in practice, owing to the complexity of the problem and the lack of sufficient evidence, such individual distributions may well remain partial or incomplete, does this show that responsibility could not in principle be exhausted by them? Presumably individuals may be responsible even if their responsibility cannot be determined by investigators. Nevertheless, I think Cooper has reasons for believing that even omniscient investigators could not exhaust the responsibility of the military system by such distributions, and these reasons have to do with his allegation that there was 'a way of life' which individual members of the military inherited when they came to Vietnam. But this, if I am correct, only shows that the options of such individuals were limited by the circumstances in which they found themselves. However, let us examine somewhat more closely how the military system in Vietnam could be held responsible, along with Lt. Calley and other individuals, for what happened at My Lai.

I cannot provide a list of necessary and sufficient conditions for holding a collective responsible for the faulty actions of some of its members, but I can perhaps do some of the reflection which would precede the creation of such a list. As I have suggested, one of the problems which My Lai illustrates is the difficulty in specifying the 'system' which is to be held responsible. Is it the US military system in Vietnam, the US military system in general, or the political system which presumably controlled and directed the US military in Vietnam? Given the ways in which systems overlap and interrelate with one another in our complex world, this problem will surely be pervasive where many ascriptions of collective responsibility are concerned. Philosophers' examples of tennis clubs and isolated frontier townships may help to illustrate the problem of collective responsibility, but there is always the risk of distortion and oversimplification if we rely too heavily on them. Assuming, however, that we can speak intelligibly of the American military system in Vietnam, the question arises as to the relation of individuals who commit faulty or wrongful actions to the system of which they are a part. Presumably, given the control which the American military has over its men, especially in a combat situation, what the individual does is closely related to the system in question, but it is just because of this unusual degree of control, by command or coercion or example, that a military system might turn out to be an atypical instance of the responsibilities of a collective.

Even in a tightly structured military system, however, individuals can do some things which need not reflect badly on it. If a drunken Lt. Calley had massacred over one hundred Vietnamese civilians while on leave in Saigon, this would not necessarily have reflected badly upon the American military system in Vietnam. Misconduct by their personnel while on leave is a problem with which all military systems have had to wrestle, and if such misconduct reflects badly on the American military system in Vietnam this might be due simply to the fact that like virtually all such systems it must rely upon youthful, restless conscripts who are taken from their homes and placed in a stressful, alien environment.

Lt. Calley in his *Autobiography* insisted that he never killed anyone, meaning that he never murdered anyone but was only following orders in a combat situation. Whether in fact he was ever ordered to destroy My Lai and its inhabitants is controversial and, of course, the 'only following orders' defense has severe limits both legally and morally where the responsibilities of individual actors are concerned. However, if such orders were given, this would reflect badly upon the American military system in Vietnam. How badly would depend upon whether Calley's immediate superior, Captain Ernest Medina, had been instructed to give such orders, and how common the issuance of such orders was. Suppose, however, as Captain Medina always insisted, no order to 'waste'm' was ever given, then perhaps Lt. Calley was truly a 'loose cannon,' which would excuse the American military system in Vietnam from some or all of its responsibility for the My Lai Massacre. Exactly how it affects the responsibility of the military depends very much on why Lt. Calley initiated the My Lai Massacre on his own. If he was a sociopath or a diabolically evil person, then there was little in the way of better psychological screening of officers or better preparation for combat that would have prevented the My Lai Massacre; even if the military was not deficient in these areas Lt. Calley would in all likelihood have slipped through the net and My Lai might have occurred anyway. But suppose, as all the evidence suggests, that Lt. Calley was an ordinary man, is he then simply an example of what has been called 'the ordinariness of evil'? Perhaps My Lai was simply the result of a decision taken by a youthful officer, nervous and inexperienced, and tragically overeager to do his duty as he saw it.

One key as to whether something like the American military system in Vietnam is to be held morally responsible is how it responds to events like the My Lai Massacre. If I am correct, the American military in Vietnam did not take adequate precautions to protect the civilian population in South Vietnam and thus contributed to the probability of an incident like My Lai occurring. This is, of course, arguable, but what is not arguable is that after the My Lai Massacre an extensive cover-up took place within the American military system in Vietnam, and that only an 'historical accident' in the form of a letter from a soldier who had been in Vietnam to members of Congress and Pentagon officials led to a significant investigation by the American military system (in the United States) into what had happened at My Lai. Eventually a commission headed by Lieutenant-General William Peers filed charges against fourteen officers ranging in rank from major-general to captain. The list of charges included failure to obey lawful regulations, dereliction of duty, false swearing, and misprision of a felony. Several promising careers, including that of a general who had by then become commandant of West Point, were ruined, but in fact only one of these officers was actually court-martialled and he was acquitted. In the other cases charges were dismissed after being reviewed by the commanding general of the First Army. Lt. Calley was tried for the My Lai Massacre and sentenced to life imprisonment, but he served only three years under house arrest before he was paroled.

In some ways the story of the cover-up is even more disturbing than My Lai itself. Calley was a raw recruit, a green officer lacking in experience and much else, someone who, it was said, could never have won a commission in peacetime. West Point graduates would never have done what Calley did, or so they were quoted as saying. Perhaps, but West Pointers lied repeatedly, and even before the Peers Commission, to protect themselves and their fellow officers. Records of several half-hearted investigations within the American Division in Vietnam were altered, and eventually some of the records disappeared from official files, taken, it was believed, by officers to protect their predecessors. No one, it seemed, wanted to know what had happened at My Lai, although from the beginning it was obvious that something had gone very wrong. Charlie Company was officially credited with killing 128 Viet Cong, but only three weapons had been found; the helicopter pilot had complained to his superiors; the Viet Cong were broadcasting stories about the massacre at My Lai within a week of its occurrence, and so on. In its investigation of the cover-up of My Lai, even the Peers Commission came to be faulted for failing 'to explore fully, not the individual actions of a few generals, colonels, and lesser officers, but an institution that made it almost inevitable that the investigations of My Lai 4 would be covered up.'[14]

Seymour Hersh concluded his story of the cover-up with a chapter with the depressing title, 'The system prevails.' On the face of it Hersh's criticism of the system is supportive of Cooper's subsequent analysis of My Lai, although the system blamed by Hersh for the cover-up seems far more extensive than the one which Cooper held responsible for what happened at My Lai. However, from the point of view of the methodological individualist, what Hersh revealed was the way in which an old boy network (a system within a system?) could limit and finally subvert the military criminal justice system (another system?). Any remedy for the sort of thing that went wrong from the initial cover-up in Vietnam to the dismissal of charges brought by the Peers Commission would be a complicated and no doubt often frustrating affair, but the direction such a remedy should take seems fairly clear. Put simply, investigations of events such as My Lai and the subsequent cover-up should be conducted not by the military but by what have come to be called 'independent prosecutors.' A superior officer in the military should not have the authority to dismiss any charges brought by these prosecutors, and trial proceedings should be automatic. To accomplish this many military rules, and attitudes, would have to be altered, so many that perhaps we might witness the emergence of a new 'way of life' in parts, if not the whole, of the American military system. But there is nothing in the nature of the system, which is after all ultimately responsible to a civilian authority, chosen by a democratic political system, which would make what is admittedly a complex reform impossible.

Where does all this leave Cooper's claim that the American military system in Vietnam was an example of collective non-distributive responsibility in the sense that although there is a distribution of responsibility over some members of this collective it does not 'exhaust' the responsibility in question? Here we can, I think, point to two components of most, if not all, systems which may be said to be 'left over' after ascriptions of individual responsibility are made. First, there are relationships among the members of a system, but the fact that Calley was a junior officer in a military hierarchy does not make the relationships between him and his superiors and the enlisted men beneath him morally responsible for what he and others did. However, such relationships will help to explain why these individuals acted as they did and may assist us in the distribution of responsibility for My Lai among (some) members of the American military system in Vietnam. Second, there are rules which define many of the relationships among members of a system, and which distribute tasks and responsibilities among such members. Some rules may be judged inadequate or indeed morally reprehensible, but it is absurd to hold a rule as such morally responsible for faulty actions by men who comply with its requirements. Thus, I conclude that what is left over in cases where ascriptions of collective responsibility are not exhausted by distributions over individual members of a system may well be 'a way of life' which consists of relationships and rules which individuals, whether deliberately or by habit or tradition, accept as members of a system. This is *not* to say that individuals such as Lt Calley and the men in Charlie Company could not have done otherwise, but it is to say that participating in such a way of life may in some circumstances count as a partially excusing condition. This would seem to be especially true when the participation is less than fully voluntary, as in the case of military conscripts or individuals such as Lt. Calley who 'volunteered' in order to avoid being drafted.

6 The responsibility of corporations

In recent years there have been two important studies of collective responsibility which have dealt with business ethics. Peter French's *Collective and Corporate Responsibility* (1984) argued that collectivism was superior to methodological individualism as a way of accounting for the responsibility of corporations. According to French, a corporation is a real person, not a fictitious entity; it just happens not to have a physical body like an individual person, but it is still a real person that can be held morally accountable for its decisions. Corporations are moral persons because they possess an internal decision structure which, according to French, means that they can form intentions and act on the basis of these intentions.[1] Larry May, in *The Morality of Groups* (1987), has argued that neither collectivism nor methodological individualism offers a viable account of collective responsibility. May rejects French's claim that a corporation is a full-fledged moral agent, but he maintains that the internal decision structure of corporations does make them morally responsible for the actions of individuals who are authorized to act on their behalf. However, French's emphasis on the importance of a collective's internal decision structure makes him unable to account for the collective responsibility of unorganized groups such as the mob that stormed the Bastille during the French Revolution. According to May, a methodological individualist such as J. W. N. Watkins is likewise unable to explain the behavior of mobs because he cannot account for the relationship of solidarity which unites their individual members and accounts for their ability to function as a group. Building upon Jean-Paul Sartre's analysis of the mob that stormed the Bastille, May maintains that its behavior was 'quasi-intentional,' although he concedes that for many members of the mob the awareness of group solidarity was 'pre-reflective.' Watkins in his explanation of the behavior of mobs had posited the existence of 'anonymous individuals,' which May criticizes as a departure from the tenets of methodological individualism, but I confess that neither Watkins nor May has advanced my own understanding of mob behavior which remains, I think, a largely unexplained phenomenon.[2] In this chapter I shall focus upon May's analysis of the collective responsibility of business corporations, whose behavior is intelligible largely because, as French and May have pointed out, they possess an internal decision structure.

I want to explore May's views on business corporations, but what he has to say about them initially involves comparing them with mobs. Business corporations and mobs are, according to May, significantly different, but they have in common the fact that the purposive conduct of the group is 'ultimately explained by reference to the group structure which itself cannot be reduced to the aggregated intentions of the individual members of the group.' Since Sartre had insisted that the mob which stormed the Bastille was unstructured, there seems to be a significant difference between him and May on this point, a difference which May overlooks when he writes: 'In the case of mobs, this structure consists of group solidarity; in the case of corporations, the structure consists of the corporate decision-making structure.'[3] I have no quarrel with May's claim that the structure of corporations consists of the corporate decision-making structure, but where mobs are concerned I think that Sartre was right and May is wrong. However, whether mobs have any discernible structure or not, it cannot be the case that this structure consists of group solidarity. May was, I think, aware that this claim was inadequate because later on he distinguished between the cohesiveness and the organization of a mob. In discussing the relationships among the members of a mob, May writes:

> Since there are no formal decision-making procedures, the cohesiveness of a mob, and hence its ability to engage in joint undertakings, is not straightforwardly a function of its organization. Rather such factors as common interests and shared beliefs about one's identity as a member of a group, as well as historical events such as the existence of a common enemy or oppressor, create a complex structure for the mob. These factors may be effective in bringing the group together in a state of solidarity.[4]

These remarks suggest that solidarity may have a number of complex causes connected with the beliefs and history of members of a mob, but they do nothing to show that a mob has any structure, complex or simple. As for May's admission that the cohesiveness and the ability of members of a mob to engage in joint undertakings is not 'straightforwardly a function of its organization,' this simply does not go far enough since (a) May has failed to show that a mob possesses any organization or structure and (b) if a mob did come to possess an organization or structure, this would seem to be more the result than the cause of its cohesiveness (although, of course, it might facilitate the mob's effectiveness in its joint undertakings). The sense, if any, in which a mob may be said to have a structure seems very different from the sense in which a business corporation may be said to have a structure because it has a decision-making structure.

It is because of its decision-making structure that May feels justified in characterizing the behavior of a corporation as fully intentional. I don't wish to belabor this point, but I see a problem here. In his analysis of mobs May suggested that intentionality and reflection are closely tied together, so that it was the pre-reflective nature of the solidarity experienced by some of its members which made the behavior of the mob 'quasi-intentional.' It seems to me that for the less reflective members of a corporation, perhaps those on the lowest rungs of the employment ladder, the intentions of the corporation may also remain pre-reflective. These lower-level employees could, perhaps, find out what the intentions (or policies) of the corporation were if they took the trouble to do so, but ordinarily they simply go about their rather limited task assignments. Unless it is corporate policy to educate all employees as to the intentions of the corporation the fact that some members remain in a state of ignorance may reduce their behavior to the 'quasi-intentional' level or, less mysteriously, simply to a level different from that of management personnel. And perhaps even if all its employees were informed about the policies, goals, and intentions of the corporation, the problem might still not be solved if they did not have at least some input into the shaping of these policies, goals, and intentions. This may help to explain a phenomenon which May neglects entirely, namely that while a corporation may in some sense be said to act intentionally it often fails to exhibit the solidarity that a mob or some other social groups may possess. The unity that a decision-making structure provides may be more formal than real, and what a corporation gains, in comparison with a mob, where structure is concerned it may lose where a sense of common purpose and commitment are concerned.

For May, the ultimate difference between the behavior of a mob and of a corporation is that the latter can be said to act *vicariously*. In making this claim May provides what is to date the most subtle challenge to methodological individualism. While French argued that, legal theory notwithstanding, a corporation is not a 'fictitious person' but is in fact a real person because it possesses a decision-making structure significantly like that of ordinary persons, May has advanced a more subtle and more plausible claim: a corporation acts for and through individual persons, and cannot act directly as individual persons can; nevertheless, because a corporation does *act* vicariously the actions of a corporation are not reducible to the actions of the individual persons who make up the corporation. As May acknowledges, the idea of vicarious agency constitutes an essential part of most traditional political theories.[5] But what is original to May is the claim that vicarious agency differs significantly in the cases of political action and corporate action.

Fundamental to May's discussion of vicarious agency is the distinction between actions of individuals in cooperation with one another and actions of individuals on the basis of power delegated to them by the corporation. Since the corporation cannot act on its own, this power is delegated by persons who are also members of the corporation.

> Could these acts have taken place without the corporate structure which is the defining characteristic of the corporate entity? Perhaps some of them could have, but they would not be describable as acts of the whole group of members of the corporation . . . . Without the 'incorporating act,' whereby the acts of different persons are linked together, certain acts could not be described as corporate acts.

The incorporating act, according to May, is the act which established a corporation and which designated the corporation as that entity which represents different persons collectively. The act of incorporation is similar to the act of voting whereby individual voters establish the office of congressman through whose agency the constituents can act collectively: 'The original stockholders, for instance, can incorporate themselves and can then act through the corporation. But the stockholders, unlike the voters, cannot truly act through the corporation without the corporation itself acting through others, its supervisors, employees, etc.'[6]

May's distinction between voters and stockholders seems unconvincing. Voters presumably create not simply the office of congressman but a government of which this office is only a part. Here there would seem to be an exact parallel with the case of original stockholders who create a corporation which includes the office of, say, chief executive officer. The alleged difference in the two cases is that the stockholders, unlike voters, cannot truly act through the corporation without the corporation itself acting through others, its supervisors, employees, and so on; but 'truly' in this case functions much like 'really' in many similar cases, and is a warning flag that some special thesis may be lurking in this claim. But if we must speak in this manner, why couldn't we say, with equal warrant, that voters cannot *truly* act through the government without the government itself acting through others, its congressmen, administrators, employees, and so on? May's reply to this sort of objection consists, I think, of two parts. First, he invokes a distinction between what Alvin Goldman has called 'object-agency' and 'event-agency.'[7] As employed by May, this turns out to be just the difference between agency on the part of individual persons and agency in the sense of the process or structure which facilitates actions by individuals. Individual agents possess object-agency, while corporations only possess event-agency. Second, May says that since corporations only possess event-agency they can only act vicariously, whereas by contrast a political representative can act both vicariously (event-agency) and directly (object-agency) on behalf of his constituents:

> Corporations can only act vicariously because they do not have object-agent status. But groups of individuals, such as the group of constituents who vote for a political representative, are different in that each of them is an object-agent, *and* the agent they act through is what Hobbes called an animate rather than an inanimate artificial person. Such a person has object-agent status and hence could properly act on his or her own and can also thereby properly represent the group directly. *The political representative is thus quite different from those who act in the name of the corporation.* The corporation cannot either authorize or act, and this is why it is, in a sense, a place-holder for those who can do one or the other of these tasks. The political

representative, unlike the corporation, acts directly in a vicarious way for his or her constituency. [My italics][8]

My response to May consists of three points.

(1) Goldman's distinction between two kinds of agency seems questionable. I cannot pursue this point in anything like sufficient detail here, but what he calls 'event-agency' is perhaps more accurately described not as a separate kind of *agency*, but simply as a set of conditions, causal or otherwise, which make it possible for individual persons to do certain things or to do them in certain ways. Without a corporate decision-making structure, for example, individual persons would not be able to declare a dividend payable to corporate stockholders.

(2) May's claim, which I italicized above, seems suspect. Of course, as I've already indicated, there is a difference between a political representative and a corporation, but no difference between a government and a corporation has been established. Even if political representatives possess object-agency and corporations possess (only) event-agency, this does not show that political representatives are 'thus' quite different from 'those who act in the name of the corporation.' In fact, I believe that political representatives and corporate representatives are on a par in that both can be said to act vicariously and directly, the political representative for his constituents and the corporate representative for his employers, the stockholders. (May's discussion of whether management because of its enormous powers can be said to control a corporation even more than its stockholders is irrelevant since a parallel discussion of the powers of government officials and voters is also possible.)

(3) Earlier May touched on the importance of act descriptions when he wrote that although some of the actions taken by individuals on the basis of powers delegated to them by the corporation could perhaps have occurred without the corporate structure — 'they would not be describable as acts of the

whole group of members of the corporation' — but in his discussion of the direct and vicarious agency of a political representative May fails to realize that exactly the same point can be made about the actions of political representatives. What the political representative could do *directly*, without or apart from the political structure, would not be describable as acts of the whole group of members of the government. For example, a congressman might investigate charges of corruption brought against the savings and loan industry, but so might a newspaperman, or any private citizen; such an investigation would not be describable as an act of the government unless the action was *authorized* by the Congress or the congressional committee of which he was a member.

Thus, so far as I can determine, May has failed to show any significant different between governments and corporations. If corporations have only indirect and vicarious (event-agency) agency, the same is true of governments; if political representatives have both direct and vicarious agency (object-agency and event-agency), the same is true of corporate representatives. Differences emerge only if a member of one of the above pairs is compared with a member of the other pair, e.g. corporations and political representatives. Either May has failed to establish his thesis about corporations or he has, unintentionally, advanced a much stronger thesis, namely that the behavior of both corporations and governments are counter-examples to the claims of methodological individualism.

May takes what he regards as a 'middle position' on the behaviour of groups, between collectivism and methodological individualism but closer to the collectivism of Peter French. As we have seen, May holds that corporations can act (indirectly and vicariously) but that only individual persons are full-fledged actors in their own right. While corporations can only act through individuals there are corporate actions which can be said to be fully intentional and which can take moral predicates. Corporate actions can be said to be fully intentional because 'the decision procedures of a corporation combine and change the intentional states of key members of the organization so as to result in purposive behavior for the group.' According to May, 'The structure of the group makes it plausible to say that there are intentions which are group-based.'[9] Members of boards of directors can pursue goals for their corporation which they would not pursue as 'isolated' individuals, and the decision-making procedure of the board can also cause individual directors to arrive at a consensus which is different from what any of them personally may have wanted for the corporation. For these reasons, May believes that the 'collective intent' of the corporation cannot be reduced to the intentions of its individual members. While May agrees with Peter French that corporations form intentions, he rejects French's claim that the corporation is an entity that has 'moral agency in its own right.' He argues that consensus among members of the board can explain why they agree to pursue a policy which none of them wanted prior to the board meeting.[10]

It is hard to know what to make of this 'middle position.' As Angelo Corlett and Victor Tam have argued, it is unclear whether the intentionality exhibited by the decision-making structure is indicative of corporate collective intentionality or the intentionality of certain powerful corporate individuals.[11] Even in situations where no single powerful corporate individual prevails in the sense of getting his way entirely, it may well be that the more powerful the individual the more he prevails over less powerful individuals. Also, one would suspect that compromises or consensuses in which no one got any of what he wanted prior to the board meeting would, in the real world, be extremely rare; in circumstances where this was not rare one would expect to find a deeply divided board of directors and in the long run perhaps an increasingly ineffectual corporation. I would tend to be suspicious of the claim that entirely new consensuses, totally different from the original preferences of all or most of the members of a board of directors, are to be expected; more typically I would expect that while, for example, the board of directors of an automobile company might be divided over whether to build more luxury cars or more economy cars, the original intention of all or most of the board members to continue building cars would prevail regardless of what consensus emerged on this particular issue.

Where consensuses, whether wholly or partly in accord with new intentions formed by members of a board of directors, do emerge, is it clear that these consensuses are caused by the decision-making structure of the corporation in question? A more commonsense explanation would be that when powerful directors A and B collide and both see that they cannot get all of what they want, they agree to compromise. This agreement reflects their relative power in the corporation and need not be, in a significant way, the result of the corporate decision-making structure. The methodological individualist might ask what, if anything, is left over once we reduce this compromise to the intentions of individual directors who find it acceptable. As to why they find a compromise acceptable, this may be because (a) it satisfies better than any attainable alternative what they want for themselves as individuals, e.g. increased control over the company or increased salaries for themselves, or (b) it satisfies better than any attainable alternative what they want for the corporation of which they are officers, e.g. an increased share of the market or an increasingly profitable product line. These considerations, of course, need not be mutually exclusive; but here one may discern two fairly distinct 'logics' of the situation, one the logic of self-interest for the individual board member, and the other the 'logic' of the collective interest of the group, in this case the corporation of which he is an influential member. Which 'logic' a particular board member chooses to accept in a given situation will depend in large part upon whether he sees himself as a self-interested individual or as a member of a group, and here many considerations, such as loyalty and commitment to a common enterprise, may come into play. Although the decision-making structure of the corporation may well place constraints upon how the individual board member can *implement* the choice he makes, I doubt that his choices can, strictly speaking, be described as being determined by the corporate decision-making structure itself. A cumbersome and inefficient procedure might make a difference in whether, for example, he thinks it worth his while to be a 'team-player,' but this is just one of many facts about his situation that he must take into account. Typically, he will, I think, be more affected by substantive considerations having to do with the cohesiveness of the board, for example, than with more formal considerations having to do with how the decisions of the board are arrived at.

May rejects both the 'collectivist' model of corporate responsibility, and the strict liability model of corporate responsibility which he attributes to Feinberg.[12] The 'collectivist' model proposes that we treat corporations as we treat individual persons in criminal law, by looking at their state of mind. This model has the advantage of preserving the fault condition as a necessary part of ascriptions of responsibility, but it suffers evidentiary problems concerning how to determine what the corporate mind is and how to separate it from the minds of individual members of the corporation. The strict liability model of corporate responsibility avoids these evidentiary problems, but it does so at the cost of neglecting questions of fault or blameworthiness. May proposes a third model of corporate responsibility which he offers as a mean between the two extremes of the 'collectivist' and strict liability models. He does this by combining vicarious agency with negligent fault, and what he says about corporate vicarious negligence is, I think, important and can stand independently of his theoretical analysis of corporate vicarious agency as a species of 'event-agency.' The model of corporate responsibility May provides is consistent with the commonsense idea, which he endorses, that the corporate entity is best seen not as a single entity but as a collection of entities or individual persons in various *relationships* with one another.

Here is May's model of corporate vicarious negligence which provides sufficient conditions for the harmful conduct

of a member of a corporation to become the responsibility of
the corporation:

A corporation is vicariously negligent for the harmful acts
of one of its members if:

(a) causal factor – the member of the corporation was
involved or facilitated in his or her harmful conduct by the
general grant of authority given to him or her by a corporate
decision; and

(b) fault factor – appropriate members of the corporation
failed to take preventive measures to thwart the potential
harm by those who could harm due to the above general
grant of authority, even though:

1. the appropriate members could have taken such precautions, and

2. these appropriate members could reasonably have pre-
dicted that the harm would occur.[13]

May maintains that the criminal act (*actus reus*) and the criminal mind (*mens rea*) of an individual corporate member can
be transferred to the corporation in cases where both the
causal factor and the fault factor of his model obtain. The
actus reus can be redescribed as an act of the corporation
because it was done under a general grant of authority under
a corporate decision. The transfer of the *mens rea* of the
individual who does the harmful act is more difficult since, as
May acknowledges, 'It is a long-standing principle in Anglo-
American law that the state of mind of a given person does
not transfer to another due to an authorization or any other
basis of vicarious agency.'[14] However, if the negligence of
corporate officers in not preventing the *actus reus* can be
established, then May believes that this will suffice to satisfy
the *mens rea* condition where the corporation is concerned.
The *mens rea* of corporate officers who fail to prevent a
harmful act need not be as serious as the *mens rea* of the

individual who actually commits the harmful act. Any related negligence by a corporate officer shows at the very least that someone besides the individual who commits the harmful act is at fault.

There is nothing original in the claim that collective responsibility is vicarious responsibility, nor is there anything especially original in May's model of corporate vicarious negligence conceived of simply as a model which explicates the factors that are involved in corporate negligence. What is original to May is his claim that his model is superior to any which conceives of corporate responsibility as a species of strict liability, and in this connection he claims that in presenting his account of corporate vicarious negligence he will make it clear why Feinberg has not given 'an adequate conceptualization of collective responsibility.'[15]

In a way, it seems remarkable for May to attach the significance that he does to his model of corporate vicarious negligence, since common sense (and the law) would suggest that negligence is but one of many possible causes of harmful acts done by individuals whether acting in their own right or on behalf of corporations. However, if we think of causation in pragmatic terms, with an emphasis upon the factors which lie within an individual's or a corporation's control, one can, I believe, argue that negligence at the very least merits special attention. According to May, his model has one minor disadvantage and one major advantage over the strict liability model. The disadvantage is that there might be an increase in the number of excuses to which a corporation would resort in its effort to show that no negligence occurred; the advantage is that, since the absence of negligence on the part of the corporate officers would now count as an excusing condition where criminal sanctions are concerned, corporations would become far more zealous in their efforts to prevent harms from occurring.[16] But what about *mens rea*? In imposing criminal sanctions upon individuals we look for both *actus reus* and *mens rea*, and what is wrong with strict liability for corporations, according to May, is that it ignores *mens rea*.

With May's model *mens rea* is satisfied when we find negligence on the part of corporate officers, and defeated when no such negligence exists. This position has a certain appeal when it is criminal and not merely civil sanctions which are involved. In tort law a penalty may be included in a contract; for example, if a building is not finished by a certain date the contractor agrees to forfeit a certain sum of money, and excuses about the weather, a possible shortage of workers, and so on simply are not recognized. But criminal sanctions are not mere penalties, nor are they the result of stipulations agreed to by certain parties to a contract; rather, they express at least symbolically the most extreme disapprobation of the community. Thus, May's corporate vicarious negligence model has the advantage of fairness: it gives a corporation a chance to explain why criminal sanctions should not be imposed.

If we employ his model here, according to May, is what would happen:

> criminal sanctions will be imposed based only on the extent of guilt [negligence] exhibited by the executives of the corporation . . . . The corporation can block the claim that it is criminally responsible by showing that there was no negligence on the part of these high-ranking managers, and thus no criminal state of mind attributable to the corporation.[17]

If May is correct, as I think he is, in the assessment of the practical implications of his model, this should give us pause before we accept it. Basically the question is one of how important negligence ought to be in determining whether criminal sanctions should be imposed on a corporation; more specifically it is a question of whether the absence of negligence is a sufficient condition for the dismissal or rebuttal of all criminal charges. Common sense suggests, I think, that things are not so simple as this, even if we grant that excuses should be allowed in some criminal cases arising from corporate misconduct. Some harms may be of such a magnitude that the absence of negligence on the part of corporate officers should not block the claim that a corporation is criminally liable for such harms, and strict liability statutes seem to reflect this judgment. Even in cases where we decide that negligence is a relevant factor its importance may be greatly affected by other considerations; for example, a little negligence by corporate officers in an enterprise with the capacity for potentially widespread and lethal harm to the public might be taken more seriously than greater negligence by corporate officers in less risky enterprises.

Suppose, however, that we were to grant May not only that the absence of negligence on the part of corporate officers might be relevant in deciding whether criminal charges should be brought against a corporation but that the absence of negligence would suffice to prevent us from bringing such charges, or if they were brought would suffice for their dismissal or rebuttal. Would this establish, as May alleges, that the conceptualization of collective liability as strict liability is wrong? I think it would show that strict liability *statutes* cannot be an adequate model for interpreting all forms of corporate liability since in crimes covered by such statutes there are no excusing conditions, but I think no one (and certainly not Feinberg) has ever supposed that strict liability statutes do supply an adequate model of all corporate liability, or that all statutes covering corporate criminality should be made over into strict liability statutes. In other words, except for strict liability statutes, excuses do already count in corporate criminal law. On the deeper issue of whether Feinberg is correct in claiming that collective liability is strict liability we should note, as May does, that Feinberg means that in ascriptions of collective responsibility the contributory fault condition which is crucial where individual liability is concerned is either weakened or absent. May's attempt to develop a model of corporate vicarious negligence is motivated by the desire to show that this is not the case, at least not always or necessarily. Yet, on May's own account, I think it is fairly clear that the contributory fault condition is at least altered where corporate vicarious negligence is concerned. The *mens rea* condition which May uses to establish corporate fault operates differently in the case of individual and corporate liability. First, states of mind cannot transfer directly. This means, I think, that the state of mind of an employee who commits a harmful act cannot be said to transfer directly either to some corporate officer or to the corporation itself, but only indirectly to the corporation by means of some mental state in a corporate officer which somehow contributes to the *actus reus* of the corporate employee. Second, not only will the state of mind of the corporate employee differ from that of the corporate officer, but it may be a more (or less) serious state of mind where *mens rea* is concerned. Thus, for example, a corporate employee may commit a harmful act fully intending that it result in harm, while a corporate officer may be at fault only in the sense of neglecting to supervise the employee's conduct as carefully as he might or should have done. Third, the state of mind of a corporate officer may become relevant only after the criminal act has occurred, i.e. in not trying or not trying hard enough to prevent its recurrence, or in trying to 'cover up' the fact that a criminal act has occurred at all. There is, as we shall see when we discuss the issue of corporate punishment, an even more serious difficulty with May's treatment of the contributory fault condition which arises from his belief that corporate intent is not reducible to individual intent. Even if we were willing to grant May that his corporate vicarious negligence model does not significantly weaken the contributory fault condition, it would be rash indeed to generalize from this model to all the models of collective responsibility cited by Feinberg. Indeed, if Feinberg and Cooper are correct, there may be cases of collective responsibility where there is a collective but non-distributive fault, i.e. cases in which the issue of negligence on the part of any member of a collective simply does not arise.

In my judgment, May's corporate vicarious negligence model has more to do with the distribution of criminal sanctions among the individual members of a corporation than with the determination of corporate responsibility as such. And, in effect, as we shall now see, this is the principal use which May himself makes of this model. In the event that corporate officers are not negligent then, according to May, the corporation should not be subject to criminal sanctions, but if they are negligent then they, not the corporation, should be punished! Although May has gone to great lengths to show that corporations can be blameworthy, he maintains that only individuals should be punished for harmful corporate acts. His reasons for this are practical and moral. On the practical level, the punishment of key individuals in high-ranking management positions will make corporate officers more zealous in the prevention of harmful corporate acts. Since their freedom and their purse will be on the line, these officers will be more motivated to prevent harmful acts by employees and low-level management. They will be less inclined to enlist the support of these employees and low-level management in cases where they might otherwise seek to use them to perpetrate or conceal corporate misdeeds. Also, on the practical level, the criminal justice system has been most successful in dealing with 'personal involvement in the commission of crimes,' and May's proposal will allow the criminal justice system to continue to focus upon individual wrongdoings, even when these occur in a corporate context. According to May, fines levied against corporations simply will not have the same deterrent effect as the punishment of corporate officers: corporations will either pass the fines on to consumers by raising prices, or will go bankrupt if the fines are too harsh and cannot be written off as the cost of doing business.[18] And here we have, I think, the basis for May's moral objection to the punishment of corporations, namely that the innocent will suffer. Either consumers who have done no wrong will be forced to pay higher prices or low-level employees who have done no wrong will be laid off. (May also considers whether courts might punish corporations by 'shaming' them, as Peter French had proposed. Courts might order corporations to pay the costs of negative publicity aimed at exposing their wrong-doing. May wisely rejects this proposal, as do Corlett and Tam, and I shall not discuss it.)

I have some objections to May's proposals, and in what follows I am greatly indebted to Victor Tam. May's practical reasons – deterrence and efficiency – for preferring the punishment of individuals for harmful corporate acts over the punishment of corporations run into serious difficulties. The principal difficulty lies with the *mens rea* requirement to which May has attached so much importance. He has tried very hard to establish that corporate intentions differ from and are not reducible to the intentions of individual members of the corporation including powerful members of the board of directors or high-level management. It is doubtful that he has succeeded in this, but in any event, I think that there is an unresolved tension between May's emphasis upon the irreducibility of corporate intentions and his insistence that corporate liability may nevertheless be satisfied by the punishment of corporate officers.[19] The problem I have in mind is this: after the *mens rea* of an employee has been 'transferred' to the corporation (via the negligence of some corporate officer), this presumably forms part of the *irreducible* intentions of the corporation. Thus, it may be unduly harsh to prosecute a corporate officer for the corporate *mens rea*, since the corporate *mens rea* is not his *mens rea*; but it may seem too slight to prosecute him only for his *mens rea*, which may after all have meant only a little inattention to detail on his part; and if this prosecution proved entirely appropriate, should we ever have bothered to determine what the corporate intentions were? Only on the assumption that May has failed to show that corporate intentions are irreducible would the prosecution of individual corporate officers but not of corporations seem to be morally warranted. I am prepared to accept the claim that corporate officers may sometimes be prosecuted since, unlike May, I am sanguine about the prospects of successful reductions of corporate intentions, but still I hesitate to join May in actually preferring the prosecution of individuals over that of cor-

porations. I would be happiest with a compromise ('a middle
position' to use May's terminology) in which individuals may
be prosecuted but usually only in conjunction with the corporation they have served. It is chiefly when corporate officers
have either exceeded their general grant of authority from the
corporation or have neglected to carry out its provisions that
their separate prosecution seems warranted, and in these
circumstances it is arguable that we are dealing only with
individual, not with corporate, wrongdoing. In other circumstances the corporation is rightly held to be liable for what
these corporate officers have done, and if this were not the
case it would be hard to understand why vicarious liability
has any importance at all.

If it is guilty individuals that May is looking for, then perhaps
he has not gone far enough. What about the stockholders on
whose behalf corporate crimes are usually committed? Of
course, the law as it now stands limits the legal liability of
stockholders to the value of the stock they hold in a corporation, but we might want to reconsider these limitations if
there is no better way to prevent criminal conduct on the part
of corporations. Where moral responsibility is concerned it
seems even safer to suggest that just as corporate officers
should become more zealous in preventing harmful acts by
low-level employees, so shareholders should become more
zealous in preventing negligence (and worse) on the part
of corporate officers. Indeed, there is already evidence of
increased moral awareness among at least some stockholders
who speak out with increasing frequency (and perhaps effectiveness) on the civic and moral responsibilities of the
corporations which after all they own. In philosophical discussions of the ways in which corporations are and are not
like real persons, it is easy to lose sight of the significance of
the legal definition of corporations as fictitious persons. As
such, the conditions of their existence are always subject in
principle to review and change by the legislature; and the
purpose of their existence, and the question of whether it is

exclusively to show a profit for stockholders, is subject to review and change by both the legislature and stockholders.

As for May's claim that court-imposed fines of corporations will be too light or too harsh, it must be conceded that this is possible, but there is no reason why it should necessarily, always, or even usually be so. Also, May is too quick in assuming that corporations could pass serious fines on to consumers simply by raising their prices. In free markets a company which attempted this might lose many of its customers to competitors who presumably are not burdened with fines. As for bankruptcy, there is genuine bankruptcy, which in many cases courts would presumably want not to happen, and which they might be able to prevent by a careful study of the resources of the company, by a 'fine tuning' of penalties matched to the company's resources, and perhaps by a payment system in which the company would not have to pay its fine all at once; and then there is a contrived bankruptcy to which May attaches an unrealistic importance. He pictures a company declaring bankruptcy solely in order to escape payment of a fine, but while this might possibly happen, it would ordinarily be a desperate last resort on the part of a company which simply could not afford to pay its fine. No one wants to lose control of his company, but this can happen to owners and managers in bankruptcy proceedings. There is a real risk that they may not regain control, and besides the fine could still be levied against the assets of the now bankrupt company. Bankrupt companies are frequently dissolved and their assets liquidated in bankruptcy proceedings, and owners and corporate officers usually want to avoid this. May writes that in the event of bankruptcy 'the corporate officers can reform themselves into a "new" corporation (chartered in a different jurisdiction) the very next day.'[20] But this is too simple, since a bankruptcy proceeding typically ties up the assets of a company, and a 'new' corporation without assets is hardly a desideratum.

According to May, 'normally, only the employees and low-level managers are hurt by bankruptcy. And yet these individuals are not necessarily the ones who were the most guilty of the crime in question.'[21] But this, also, is too simple: investors may lose their money, and high-level corporate officers may lose their jobs when their company goes bankrupt. As May notes, corporate officers may find employment elsewhere, but the same is true of employees and low-level managers. While undergoing a court-ordered reorganization a bankrupt company may continue to operate under a court-appointed trustee, with the result that employees and low-level managers may well retain their jobs indefinitely. Nevertheless, May makes an interesting point, namely that those who may be innocent, totally or in large part, of contributing to criminal wrongdoing by a corporation may suffer, and under some circumstances may even suffer the most. But is this a decisive reason not to impose criminal sanctions on a corporation? I think it is not, especially if we value deterrence as much as May clearly does. The knowledge that they may be laid off might well turn employees and low-level managers into zealous guardians of product quality and related matters, just as May expected the fear of criminal sanctions to turn corporate officers into zealous overseers of what goes on in the work place.

If, however, we leave aside the question of deterrence and focus on the fairness of lay-offs which may result from bankruptcy, this issue can be troublesome. How much suffering these lay-offs may cause depends upon variables such as the availability of jobs with other companies; it may also be argued that employees' suffering is tied to some extent to their expectations. Academics such as May and I have high expectations where job security is concerned, but factory workers may have much lower expectations. Even highly trained professionals such as engineers often have little prospect of job security in volatile industries like aerospace. Still, unemployment can be traumatic, and there are divorce, alcoholism, and suicide statistics which underscore that self-esteem is intimately tied to whether one has a job. Causally, while a defective product may actually be made or released by a low-level employee, he is often acting 'under orders' from someone higher up in the corporation; many low-level employees often have no role, causal or otherwise, in the harmful actions which form the basis for the prosecution of corporations. Still, on the score of fairness May's insistence that corporate officers, not corporations, be punished overlooks one important consideration, namely who is to pay for corporate wrongdoing. Presumably, this question may be answered in part by civil proceedings directed against the corporation. May's silence on this point leads me to suspect that his objection is only to criminal sanctions against corporations, not to civil penalties although these could also force a company into bankruptcy and its workers into unemployment. My point is simply that someone should have to pay for corporate wrongdoing, and that typically corporate officers, while well-to-do, could not begin to cover the cost of compensating the victims of at least the more serious cases. So we may be in a situation where rights, or claims to rights, collide: victims' rights to compensation versus employees' rights to a job. However this is resolved, the innocent will suffer. If workers do suffer as a result of the criminal sanctions directed against their employers, this is not the intent behind such sanctions but it is arguable that corporate wrongdoing is usually intended to enrich the corporation and frequently does so by violating consumers' rights to safe products or citizens' rights to a clean environment. Whether these violations are the result of conspiracy or negligence – and the two may not be as much alike as May claims in his corporate vicarious negligence model – is really beside the point, since either way a corporation may be liable to criminal as well as civil penalties.

If a corporation goes bankrupt following criminal sanctions, and employees and low-level management do lose their jobs, the responsibility for this rests squarely upon the corporation, not on the criminal justice system. This case is partially analogous with that of an individual criminal who is punished by the criminal justice system: if his family suffers loss of income and status as a result, then he is responsible, not the criminal justice system. But why should the corporation and not key management personnel bear the brunt of criminal sanctions? Because the corporation is vicariously responsible for harmful acts done in its name, especially when these acts have been encouraged or tolerated by its management. There are three reasons why punishment may be justified: its deterrent effect, its fairness to the parties involved, and its symbolic significance. Where deterrence is concerned, it has not been shown that limiting the punishment for corporate harmful acts to high-level officers will be more effective than punishing the corporation. On the level of fairness, criminal sanctions against a corporation would only be significantly unfair if employees and low-level management personnel who had done no wrong lost their jobs, but the other considerations indicated above suggest that on balance fairness is best served by the punishment of the corporation. Finally, there is the symbolic function of punishment about which I have said nothing and which is difficult to evaluate. Punishment is the most severe expression of disapproval available to a community when one of its members has acted wrongfully against another of its members, or against the entire community. In the case of corporations which for certain restricted purposes are treated as members of the community and which are allowed special privileges which individual persons do not enjoy, punishment is a reminder that the corporation exists subject to certain rules laid down by the community and that it is subject to punishment just as if it were an individual person when these rules are violated. As May points out, corporations cannot be put in jail, and cannot feel or experience shame in the way that a real person can, but these differences do not in my judgment suffice to exempt them from punishment. Although they cannot be imprisoned, their freedom to operate in certain ways can be curtailed, and their charters can be revoked. Corporations cannot be made to feel shame, as Peter French thought they could (on the ground that they are real persons), but the owners, managers, and employees of corporations certainly can. Just as these individuals can take pride in the production of a superior product and its success in the marketplace, and can feel shame at commercial failures, so they can be shamed by criminal sanctions brought against the corporation. And whether they are ashamed or not, the community has served notice of its disapproval. Since individual officers, employees, and stockholders may come and go, criminal sanctions against a corporation more adequately express public disapproval of the ways in which business has been done by that corporation and serve notice perhaps that this kind of sub-standard conduct will not be tolerated in the future. Corporations no less than individuals can acquire a 'bad name' and be made to suffer the consequence.

There is, I think, a surface paradox in the different positions May and I take on the issue of corporate punishment. May, who claims that his 'middle position' is actually closer to that of the collectivist, would punish individuals, not corporations; while I, an unabashed methodological individualist, would punish corporations, although I would sometimes punish individual members of the corporation as well. But this is only a surface paradox, since I believe that corporations are only (nothing but) groups of individuals organized in certain ways. Corporations are undoubtedly complex groups, consisting as they do of stockholders, managers, and employees, but in my judgment stockholders as the owners of a corporation should, and at present do, usually bear the brunt of any criminal sanctions directed against corporations. Criminal sanctions in the form of fines, provided they are severe enough, can adversely affect the amount of dividends and the value of stocks held by stockholders. If other members of a corporation, employees or low-level managers for example, suffer as a result of criminal sanctions against it, this should be regarded as an unintentional effect of such sanctions. However, because it may under certain conditions be foreseeable, the legislature may wish to take actions aimed at alleviating the suffering of these unfortunate victims of corporate wrongdoing; such actions may take the form of, for example, unemployment insurance, job retraining and relocation programs.

7 The distribution of liability

Feinberg writes that 'group liability is inevitably distributive: what harms the group as a whole necessarily harms its members.' This judgment occurs in the context of a discussion of non-distributive group fault where Feinberg concedes that 'one would think that where group fault is non-distributive, group liability must be so too, lest it fall vicariously on individual members who are faultless.'[1] There seems to be a dilemma here: either we have to accept ascriptions of group liability even though they may result in harm to individuals who are not at fault, or else the whole point of talking about collective actions and group responsibility for these actions is lost. One way around this dilemma would be to try to make ascriptions of group liability more morally palatable, and I regard May's *The Morality of Groups* as an important though flawed step in this direction.[2] On May's analysis, corporations may be blameworthy for certain wrongdoings, but only corporate officers should be punished for them. This is in accord with the widely held conviction that where there is wrongdoing we should try to pick out the individual wrongdoers, but it fails, I think, to do full justice to the idea of vicarious collective responsibility. Even in cases where there is no evidence of vicarious corporate negligence, a corporation may be vicariously responsible for wrongs done 'in its name.' Still, in its efforts to drive a wedge, as I see it, between ascriptions of liability and the distribution of actual punishment, May's book represents an important pioneering effort, and I wish now to explore further some of the ways in which the seeming harshness of ascriptions of collective liability could be alleviated.

It might, of course, be objected that there is no difference between ascriptions of liability and punishment, but this is clearly wrong. Liability is liability to punishment, or in some cases liability to moral censure; and the difference I have in mind between ascriptions of liability and actual punishment corresponds to the two phases typical of most criminal proceedings: first, there is the determination of guilt which results in a conviction; then there is the sentencing of the party found guilty. These two phases may or may not involve two separate proceedings, but even in the case of automatic sentencing they are logically separate and distinct. Even if it is true, as Feinberg maintains, that what harms the group as a whole necessarily harms its members, it is a fact of experience that what harms the group as a whole does not necessarily harm all its members in the same way. Harm, as May points out, may sometimes fall most heavily upon group members who least deserve it and can least afford it. If this is a state of affairs we wish to avoid or minimize, then there are two basic ways in which we might proceed. First, we might attempt to show: (a) that some putative members of a group are not to be counted as members of the group; or (b) that, while the group as a whole is liable to punishment, certain individual members of the group are not guilty of wrongdoing. Second, during the 'sentencing' phase when penalties are imposed upon the group, we might attempt to see that their impact falls most heavily upon those who most deserve them and to avoid as far as possible severely penalizing members of the group who are not guilty of wrongdoing. Both of these strategies undoubtedly involve practical and moral difficulties which may limit what we can hope to accomplish. Picking out which individuals are not to be counted as members of a group may be difficult and the results may be vulnerable to charges of being *ad hoc* and arbitrary; and the imposition of penalties designed to have different impacts upon selected individuals or sub-groups within a group may require some very complicated social engineering and lead to some seemingly unwarranted interference with the group's internal affairs, e.g. in telling a corporation who can and cannot be discharged. Although serious, these difficulties do not seem to me insuperable, and I think that my proposed strategies may help to make ascriptions of collective liability more morally acceptable. As an amendment to Feinberg I suggest the following (slogan): although group liability is necessarily distributive, it is still up to us to decide who is a member of a group and to determine how penalties are to be applied to a group.

Group membership may not seem all that problematic; after all, people 'vote with their feet,' that is, they can leave a country or resign from a corporation. But things may not always be as simple as this suggests. For example, the time of a departure may be crucial in determining a person's motive for ceasing to be a member of some political or corporate group. Did he leave in protest over some collective wrongdoing or because he saw the 'writing on the wall' and wanted to leave before penalties were applied to the group in question? Perhaps we could in some cases set a cut-off point and say that anyone who did not leave before that date would still be considered a member of a group. Also, we might be able to agree that anyone who joined after a certain date would not be counted as a member of the group, the ground for this exemption being that the wrongdoing in question had occurred prior to his joining. It might be possible to go even further with our list of exemptions, at least in the political sphere where we sometimes encounter alienated sub-groups and resistance movements bent upon overthrowing the 'establishment'. But what about the corporate sphere where we might, for example, encounter 'good' corporate officers who had tried to prevent negligence and other forms of corporate wrongdoing? Here, however, since these individuals continued to serve as corporate officers, presumably to their own considerable benefit, it would perhaps be best not to attempt to treat them for certain purposes as non-members but simply to declare that although they are members of the corporation they are without (any relevant) fault and are not personally guilty of any wrongdoing.

My second strategy suggests that we try as far as possible to align penalties against a group with faulty performances by individuals in such a way as to have the least impact upon those who contributed the least, or did not contribute, to the wrongdoing in question. To the extent that we could predict the impact of the various penalties, we might be able to select just those which would best serve the purposes stated above. In some cases we might leave nothing to chance and state explicitly the court's intention regarding the *distribution* of the impact of the penalties. To do this we might perhaps have to get the legislature to broaden the discretionary powers of the courts, but this ought to be possible. Armed with such powers, the courts might then inform a corporation, for example, that certain fines should be paid by the company out of its cash reserves or at the expense of stockholders' dividends rather than from savings generated by the lay-off of those corporate officers who had struggled to prevent the wrongdoing or of low-level management and employees who played no part in it.

In some cases the criminal justice system might still be too blunt an instrument for imposing the morally optimal sanctions in just the right way, but I cannot foresee any reason why it should not succeed in many cases. Of course, there is nothing in the two strategies that I have proposed which would rule out the possibility of additional criminal proceedings being taken against individual members of corporations for their contributory role, causal or otherwise, in corporate wrongdoing. But the point of my two proposed strategies is that while group liability is necessarily distributive this should be seen as the beginning and not the end of the story, and that we need to take a more active part in determining how the distribution of the liability through penalties is to be done. Success in this endeavor, whether by the use of my proposed strategies or by some other means, would, I think, go a long way toward 'winning over' those who are concerned that ascriptions of collective liability weaken or ignore the conditions we insist upon where determinations of individual liability are concerned.

May writes that 'corporations resemble conspiracies in that there is a common agreement among a group of people to engage in a certain type of behavior toward a certain end.'[3] However, it is equally true that corporations resemble churches and country clubs for the very same reason; but the resemblance May has in mind takes on significance when, in defending his model of vicarious corporate negligence, he writes that typically cases of corporate negligence turn out to involve some kind of conspiracy. He cites the case of *United States v. Park* in which John R. Park, the president of Acme Markets, Inc., was found criminally liable for, in the words of the court, 'causing the adulteration of food' which had been stored in Acme warehouses and sold in Acme Markets. The Food and Drug Administration had twice informed Park that his Baltimore warehouses contained rodents, and he had not acted to correct this unsanitary condition. Park's defence was that he had not caused the unsanitary conditions to obtain and that his only responsibility lay in selecting 'dependable subordinates' to correct the problem. I agree tentatively with May that this case does resemble a conspiracy in that the supervisory personnel and Park apparently did little or nothing to correct the unsanitary conditions even after being informed of them by the Food and Drug Administration. My opinion is that prior to notification by the Food and Drug Administration Park had arguably discharged his responsibilities by selecting subordinates whom he believed to be dependable, but that after notification, especially after the second notification, he should have realized that they were not dependable, and thus he allowed an unsafe and illegal condition to continue. One can only conclude that Park himself was not especially dependable. But does all this amount to conspiracy? Where criminal culpability is concerned there is an adverbial hierarchy of sorts, which runs from 'purposefully' through 'knowingly'

on down to 'recklessly' and 'negligently' causing or contributing to wrongdoing; and I believe that criminal conspiracy
requires, or should require, that at least some members of a
conspiracy must act purposefully, although others may only
act knowingly, in the sense of knowing what their co-conspira-
tors are about. It would, I think, be unfounded to assert that
either the supervisory personnel or Park acted purposefully to
create, or permit, unsanitary conditions to obtain in Acme
warehouses, although presumably the supervisory personnel
knew, or should have known, about these conditions even
prior to the intervention of the Food and Drug Administration.
It would, I think, also be unfounded to assert that after being
warned by the Food and Drug Administration Park and his
subordinates got together and agreed to ignore or defy its
advice. Park argued that he instructed his subordinates to see
to it that the warehouses were cleaned up, and he had no
doubt that they would do so. Park's action may seem reasonable, given his (mistaken) assumption that his subordinates
were reliable, but they apparently did little, if anything, to
correct the problem and Park, because of his position, was
held criminally liable for causing the adulteration of food in
Acme warehouses. Acme Markets, Inc. was also held criminally liable for what was done (or not done) on its behalf.
However, while this is perhaps a classic case of corporate
negligence and negligence by a corporate officer, is it a case
of conspiracy? While it does resemble a conspiracy in that
Park and his subordinates did not adequately address a problem which they knew existed, there is no evidence that they
acted in concert to ignore or to defy the warnings from the
Food and Drug Administration. It may be said that the parties
involved acted knowingly, but no one seems to have acted
purposefully to ignore or to defy these warnings. (I suspect that
Park's subordinates did as Park had done, i.e. they 'passed
the word' on down through the 'chain of command' without
personally checking to see if the problem had in fact been
solved.) Thus, in my judgment, this case is not a bona fide
example of a criminal conspiracy.

Even if it were a case of conspiracy, it would still differ from more standard examples in some important respects. First, as May points out, corporations 'normally' aim at what is legal, and conspiracies 'by definition' aim at what is illegal. Second, conspiracies in the corporate sphere usually occur *within* a corporation, whereas criminal conspiracies typically are conspiracies *of* a band of conspirators. Acme Markets, Inc. was legally engaged in the business of selling food and was not accused of any conspiracy to sell adulterated food; also, the stockholders and the vast majority of its employees, including initially Mr Park, were not aware that some Acme foods were subject to contamination by rodents. Thus, if there had been any conspiracy it would have been restricted to a relatively small number of employees, and in this case the 'conspiracy' would have partaken more of recklessness or negligence than of any purposeful disregard of public safety. How different this is from the case of a band of conspirators planning to rob a bank, for example; here every member has some part to play in the undertaking and none can plead ignorance of what was going on, though knowledge of crucial details may not have been disseminated by the gang leaders except on a 'need to know' basis.

Now for my more serious proposal. Corporations resemble nation states far more than they resemble conspiracies in that, while they are engaged in a certain type of behavior toward a certain end, not all their members are actively involved in the commission of a wrongful act or are even aware that a wrongful act has occurred. Nation states may, for example in wartime situations, sometimes resemble a conspiracy in the sense of exhibiting a certain singlemindedness in the pursuit of a common goal such as a military victory, but typically nation states are more 'pluralistic' in terms of their behavior and goals than a conspiracy would be. Typically, when wrong-doing is attributable to a nation state, even in wartime not all members of the state are actively involved in its commission, nor are they always aware that a wrongful act has occurred. I do not propose to undertake a systematic comparison of nation states and corporations, which would involve an examination of questions such as the extent to which membership in these organizations is voluntary. Presumably, though we speak of 'wage slaves' and 'economic necessity,' it is usually easier to change one's job than it is to change one's country; and, of course, some nation states bring considerable coercive pressure to bear upon their members to keep them from migrating. But the main resemblance I have in mind is simply this: vicarious liability may in both cases fall upon the organization and be distributed over all its members, even those who have had no part in some particular wrongdoing. Even when there are conspiracies within a nation state or a corporation to commit a wrongful act these usually fall far short of involving all of the members of the nation state or corporation; this, of course, raises questions of fairness where the distribution of liability is concerned. There is, of course, a difference in how corporate liability and national liability are characterized. Whether or not corporations normally aim at what is legal, they operate subject to certain legal constraints, and their liability in cases where these constraints are violated is usually to some form of punishment. In the international realm, while there are constraints in the form of treaties and covenants, when these are violated by a nation state there is usually no liability to legal punishment by a coercive device; that is, there is as yet no international criminal justice system comparable to those which operate within nation states. Here it may be relevant to recall the old Roman principle, *nullum crimen sine lege* (no crime without a law); however, there may be 'moral crimes' in the absence of laws and legal sanctions, and thus it may still make sense to speak of the liability of nation states, even though this is not usually characterized as liability to punishment. Nation states may be subject to liability of many sorts: to moral censure, to demands for apologies and reparations, to economic sanctions, and to political and military counter-measures. Thus, if I am correct, what has been said about the liability of corporations to punishment, and the moral problems it gives rise to, may help to illuminate the moral liability of nation states.

What results, if any, do the preceding discussions of military and corporate responsibility yield where the issue of terrorism is concerned? Let me begin by recalling my definition of terrorism as an attempt to bring about political, social, economic or religious change by the actual or threatened use of violence. I also noted that such use of violence was intended to publicize the cause represented by the terrorists who rarely, if ever, expect their use of violence to bring about, by itself and in a direct manner, the political or social change they seek. It is often and correctly said that terrorism is a weapon of the weak against the strong, and the violence employed by terrorists, while it may destabilize and inconvenience, is usually not sufficient to topple any 'establishment.' The successes terrorism has realized thus far have in my judgment been mainly at the expense of a dying colonialism, e.g. against the French in Algeria, the British in Kenya, and the British in Israel. Here the colonialism was not, especially toward the end, the reflection of any unanimous consensus within the ruling power, but was rather a source of moral discomfort to an increasing number of its citizens. Although terrorism increased the cost in money and lives which the continuation of colonialism required, it finally succeeded by helping to convince public opinion in the ruling power that the policy of denying the right of self-determination to subject peoples was unjust. Thus, we have this seeming paradox: terrorism by its use of methods widely perceived as unjust has helped to bring about results widely perceived as just. There is, of course, no iron law of history which shows that terrorism will always or usually have such results. If, for example, the Red Brigade had caused the democratically elected government of Italy to fall, and be replaced by a totalitarian regime representing either the extreme left or the extreme right, this would in my judgment have been a moral tragedy, but it is not, I think, an historical accident that nothing like this has yet occurred.

This suggests that there may be very real historical limitations as to what terrorism can accomplish. Wars and revolutions have frequently toppled democratically elected governments, but not once has terrorism achieved this result. (The ousted colonial powers cited above had democratically elected governments at home, but that is, of course, another matter.) The key to the limits of terrorism lies in the fact that it is the last resort of the weak; the strong apparently do not need it: wars and revolutions are their stock in trade. Only by its impact upon public opinion, an opinion already divided and at least partially disposed to accept the position championed by the terrorists, has terrorism achieved its successes to date. (Sometimes the impact has been on public opinion within a country, and sometimes, at least initially and in large part, on 'world opinion,' which has then affected domestic public opinion. Arguably, something like this has happened in South Africa with its democratically elected government chosen by whites in a society where blacks were not permitted to vote. South Africa has seen some limited terrorism directed by blacks against an oppressive white regime, and considerable 'state terrorism' directed by this regime against the black majority.) However, if terrorism has not as yet toppled a democratically elected government, it has sometimes brought about significant political and social change within a society with a democratically chosen government. A case in point might be the terrorism of the IRA. Instead of provoking extreme counter-measures it has instead helped to induce the British government to take steps to lessen discrimination against Catholics in Northern Ireland. The issue here is enormously complicated, since it is disputed whether Great Britain should be considered a colonial power clinging to its last foothold or as the government of choice favored by a majority of the people of Northern Ireland. The motivation of the British government in acting against discrimination may have been at once practical and moral, both lessening the appeal of the IRA and rectifying an historical injustice.

Punishment seems essentially connected to the existence of

institutions, especially a criminal justice system; within that criminal justice system, at least typically, only individuals who have certain clearly designated roles may punish other individuals. Policemen may arrest, prosecutors may bring charges, but only judges and juries can determine whether individuals are guilty of those charges and what, within certain statutory limits, the defendants' punishments will be; then it is up to other designated members of the criminal justice system, e.g. prison personnel, to see that the punishment is carried out. Apparent counter-examples, such as the punishment of children by their parents, can, I believe, be explained (away) by the acknowledgment that in most legal systems the family is considered a special institution. Parents enjoy a certain autonomy as to how their offspring will be treated, and are granted certain broad discretionary powers in keeping with their unique responsibilities for the upbringing of their children; but even here there are legal constraints on what punishments parents may impose, and the criminal justice system (one institution) may be authorized to intervene in the workings of another institution (the family) to protect the rights of children. All of the above may be read as a preamble to a relatively simple point, namely that terrorists cannot, strictly speaking, be said to punish anyone, simply because they lack the requisite legal powers or authority. 'State terrorism' may seem to be a counter-example, but often terrorism by a state against some of its citizens is an extra-legal activity. It is true that some of the anti-Semitic activities of the Nazi government were apparently legal in that there were statutory enactments covering them. But this is a curious anomaly since the statutes were enacted in secret and not published. Thus, if it is a requirement that a law in order to be a law must be publicized, the mistreatment of Jews under these statutes must have been of questionable legality. However, I believe that terrorists may enjoy something very much like a right to punish individuals or groups of individuals under certain rather special circumstances. Picture here a terrorist organization somewhat along the lines of 'a government in exile.' Here the 'government' in question may pronounce certain individuals or groups guilty of certain 'crimes' against the group it represents, and terrorists may be dispatched to carry out 'punishments' against them. Boundaries of jurisdiction cannot be decisive here because they may be precisely or in part what is at issue between the terrorists and their adversaries. But on the model of the nation state, going beyond a nation's boundaries to apprehend or punish 'criminals' is not always illegal; at least so Israel argued where the apprehension of Adolf Eichmann and other war criminals was concerned, and the government of the United States has taken a similar position over the apprehension and even punishment of terrorists and drug traffickers. But let us ignore the complications arising from state terrorism and terrorism conceived along the lines of 'a government in exile,' and grant the basic point that terrorists, because they lack any generally recognized legal right to punish, cannot be said to be in a position actually to punish anyone. Even so, it would not follow that our discussion of legal liabilities with reference to the military and to corporations cannot be illuminating in the construction of a rationale justifying terrorism under certain circumstances. After all, what was said about legal liabilities was in reference to their moral justification and the moral problems they may give rise to.

Liability, whether to punishment or other negative responses, arises typically because some harm has been done or threatened. Liability, when it is morally justifiable, is usually so because the harm in question is not simply a set-back to an interest but a set-back to an interest to which the 'injured party' has a right. Morally justifiable ascriptions of liability may occur whenever a rights violation takes place. Vicarious liability arises when a representative of a group, acting as such, and not as an individual pursuing his own objectives, has committed a harmful act; ascriptions of vicarious liability to a group are justifiable when the harmful act in question is also a rights violation. Such justifiable ascriptions of liability fall upon a group and all its members. Why is this so? Roughly, I think, because members of a group typically stand to benefit from belonging to it: it is in their interest to belong, or else they would not, though, of course, this assumes that membership is voluntary. In cases where membership is not voluntary, then of course the picture changes significantly, but the burden of proof, I think, falls upon the member to show that his membership was not voluntary. Since few if any of our choices are fully voluntary, what usually has to be shown is that there was some coercive element which excuses membership and which, if sufficiently strong, may negative membership altogether. But the coercion, I think, has to be a deliberate and intentional act by some would-be coercer; 'natural necessity' or 'economic necessity' would not by themselves suffice.

Just as membership has to be handled gingerly, so does benefit. The benefit must be tied in with an interest which group membership will advance, and it is not enough to point to a benefit in which a member is simply not interested. And, of course, not all those in a group need expect to secure the same benefits from their membership. What is crucial here is not whether membership actually will advance the interests of members but their subjective expectations: mistaken beliefs cannot be allowed to negative the importance of perceived prospective benefits. Also, benefits have to be tied to membership in such a way as to allow for those which are to the advantage of a member under a certain description only; that is, we must allow for a benefit which may involve a set-back to some of the interests of a member. Thus, for example, membership in a labor union may benefit a worker as a self-conscious member of the proletariat, while not advancing and in some cases actually setting back his interests as a breadwinner for his family. Thus, interest, benefit, and membership cannot be fettered unduly by narrow calculations having to do with self-interest conceived of in terms of some economic model of rationality.

Let us define liability as liability to sanctions where sanctions are a genus of which punishment, moral censure, etc., are species. The important thing here is, I believe, that once ascriptions of liability are seen as warranted it is up to us, subject to certain constraints, to decide what kind of liability and what sanctions are appropriate. Having acted wrongfully, a person or a group becomes vulnerable to a variety of negative responses which simply could not come into play, morally speaking, if a wrongful act had not been committed. Where the criminal justice system is concerned there are two principal rationales for punishment, i.e. retribution and deterrence; but moral philosophers, for the most part, tend to be happier with the latter. Retribution, whatever its virtues, increases the amount of suffering in the world, and unless it serves the end of deterring individuals or groups from further wrongdoing it scarcely seems an edifying spectacle, however much the offender may 'deserve' to be punished. The criminal justice system may serve to deter further wrongdoing simply by 'striking fear' into the hearts of all citizens, but if it is to have the moral support of the majority it must operate subject to certain constraints having to do with the appropriateness and reasonableness of the punishments it imposes. A criminal justice system which punished (or 'punished') randomly and arbitrarily would lose the respect upon which its long-term success in deterring crime would most likely depend. (How, as some commentators have asked recently, can we respect a criminal justice which allows for the execution of the mentally retarded?) Thus, it would seem that, while retribution as an end in itself would prove hard to defend, as a means to the end of deterrence it may be indispensable; that is, only if punishment is directed against wrongdoers (a retrospective consideration) can the end of deterring wrongdoing (a prospective consideration) be advanced − unless, of course, we opt for a totalitarian system in which people come to expect the criminal justice system to be unjust and plan their lives, as best they can, accordingly.

In the case of terrorism, for reasons that I have indicated, the very idea that terrorists can *punish* anyone seems, by definition, out of place, but terrorism and the criminal justice system nevertheless have certain significant resemblances, both being aimed at eliminating or reducing certain perceived injustices in the world. Of course, the criminal justice system is an institution already in place and widely, though not universally, respected, whereas terrorism can as yet hardly be said in any significant sense to be an institution (in the sense of a rule-governed activity) and it is widely, though not universally, condemned. However, with the criminal justice system as an imperfect model, it might be possible to devise some rules for the, as it were, institutionalization of terrorism, or if that is too tall an order, at least a list of some conditions which might help us to determine whether some particular terrorist act is morally justifiable, and hence worthy of some measure of respect.

Terrorists who reflect morally upon their position must ask the question of how to bring about the end of an injustice being done by some group. And, broadly speaking, the answer must be to decrease the benefits and increase the burdens of membership in the group responsible for the injustice. These burdens can be increased by harms inflicted upon members of the group in question and by publicizing its unjust behavior. In our world where there are so many demands upon us a terrorist action may be the only or the most efficient way of calling attention to some injustice that needs rectifying. Terrorism, of course, differs in kind from civil disobedience which is essentially non-violent, but both activities involve breaking the law as a means of publicizing what the participants believe to be an injustice. Both the terrorist and the practitioner of civil disobedience engage in an activity which will at least initially be met with disapproval from many people and may provoke strong counter-measures. Both the terrorist and the practitioner of civil disobedience resort to their illegal activities only after rational discourse and democratic procedures, if any, have failed to bring about the political or social change they seek. Practitioners of civil disobedience remain, however, essentially optimistic that, by their willingness to suffer the penalties attached to their action, they can touch the hearts of people including their oppressors in such a way as to persuade them to undertake the needed reforms. By contrast, terrorists are not nearly so sanguine about the prospect of change, and their tactics reflect a desperation largely unknown to the practitioner of civil disobedience. Their resort to force or violence is aimed more at the intimidation or coercion of the oppressor, but mainly they hope by attracting attention to their cause to affect public opinion in such a way that repugnance over what they have done will in time give way to sympathetic comprehension of why they have done it. In Chapter 1 I gave self-defense against genocide as one cause that might make terrorism morally acceptable, but in fact terrorism in our time has probably been more concerned with the right to national self-determination than with any other single cause. Here the terrorist must know that we in the West at least, with our history of wars and revolutions fought in large measure for our right to self-determination, cannot be entirely blind to the fact that other nations, even those partly or wholly unaffected by the liberal, democratic values which inspired our struggles for independence, also have this right. Thus, terrorists active in the cause of national liberation have some reason to hope that what they are doing may help to bring about a favorable assessment or re-evaluation of their cause. Terrorists active on behalf of other causes, such as religious fundamentalism or political extremism of the left or right, have less reason to believe that public opinion in the West will respond favorably to them; and their hopes for success, if any, may lie in their ability to destabilize governments lacking a broad base of public support, and in an appeal to emotions and values which have not prevailed in the West but might prevail or come to be intensified elsewhere.

With these considerations in mind, let us see how the model of the criminal justice system might affect our conception of terrorism. One thing that cannot fail to impress students of the foundations of the criminal justice system is just how much social engineering of a piecemeal nature has gone into its construction. Strict liability laws would be an obvious example of such social engineering: manufacturers, food processors, and bankers, for example, can all be held criminally liable for faulty products or activities even when the parties involved did not knowingly or deliberately act in a wrongful manner. If it is true that much of the injustice in the world is done by people who are simply not aware that what they are doing is unjust, then the strict liability provisions of our criminal justice system may be relevant to the issue of terrorism. The terrorist, having witnessed the failure of conventional procedures to persuade public opinion that an injustice exists, may proceed to take more drastic measures as a way of (a) increasing public awareness that there is an injustice which needs rectifying, and (b) imposing penalties for the continued failure to rectify this injustice. Strict liability statutes make it clear that where wrongdoings which have a significant impact upon the public welfare and safety are concerned, 'ignorance is no excuse.' Or, more precisely, ignorance is no excuse where the determination of liability is concerned, but usually the actual punishment is less severe than in cases of deliberate or knowing wrongdoing. Thus, one of the first questions that 'morally concerned' terrorists must consider is whether the injustice they wish to correct is the result of some deliberate or knowing activity, such as genocide, or whether it is more like the kinds of wrongdoing covered by strict liability statutes. This is important because the severity of terrorists' activities would presumably be affected by how they would answer this question. Of course, it would be easy to scoff and say that terrorism is all of a piece and does not admit of the kinds of distinctions we find in the criminal justice system, but this on close inspection seems not to be the case. While the standard picture of terrorism, propagated by the media, is that it is simply a species of moral craziness or fanaticism which is incapable of making distinctions, this seems not to fit the facts. For example, the vast majority of terrorist activities are 'crimes' against property, not against persons. This may to some extent simply reflect a strategy of striking where the risk of getting caught is lower, but it can, or should, reflect moral considerations to do with the appropriateness of the harm inflicted, its 'educational' value as a reminder, and so on. Here I assume that terrorists, not unlike the criminal justice system, are, or should be, more interested in deterrence than in retribution; and in strict liability statutes we see a precedent for imposing penalties that are aimed primarily at deterrence rather than retribution. And, of course, as I have argued above, strict liability statutes do not begin to exhaust the various ways in which the criminal justice system may deal with collective responsibility.

This book has been written to make a case for the thesis that terrorism may under certain circumstances be morally justifiable. To distinguish terrorist activities from (merely) criminal activities, I have introduced considerations to do with collective responsibility for certain injustices done by the groups against which terrorism is directed. Suppose, however, that the tables are turned, and that the injustices alleged by the terrorists simply are not injustices after all. Then, of course, the considerations to do with the collective responsibility of groups may be turned against the terrorists and the groups which they represent or which support them. If I am correct, it is in the final analysis all a question of justice, though tempered not so much by mercy as by various prudential considerations. Decisions about liability, whether it be to punishment, to moral censure, or to violence, reflect, or should reflect, more basic decisions about the kind of world we wish to live in. Ideally, of course, most of us would opt for a world in which there was no violence of any sort but, living in the real world, many of us have agreed that a limited amount of violence in the cause of justice may be permitted and in some cases required. (Even Gandhi said that if he were limited to a choice between engaging in violence and accepting what he called 'emasculation' he would opt for violence.) Opponents of the violence associated with terrorism need to ask hard questions about the justice of their own institutions, especially as they affect minorities at home and weaker nations abroad. Terrorists, on the other hand, when convinced of the justice of their cause, need to select morally appropriate targets and to avoid where possible indiscriminate violence.

Karl Marx remarked that the bombings by Sinn Fein would cause them to lose the support of the British working class, many of whose members might otherwise have been sympathetic to the cause of Irish independence. This seems to have been only a tactical observation on his part, but it can without difficulty be made into a strong moral point, especially in view of what I have said about collective responsibility. While all members may be vicariously responsible for what a group has done, some members, usually those in a position of power within the group, may be at fault for particular wrongs and injustices done by the collective. While liability for collective wrongdoing or injustice falls upon an entire group, the distribution of liability in the form of penalties may affect some of its members more than others. In view of these considerations, terrorists should take as much care as possible to avoid harming those individual members of a group who have played no part in some collective wrongdoing or injustice; terrorists should also as a matter of prudence avoid harming actual or potential believers in the justice of their cause. Ordinarily, 'morally concerned' terrorists who have reflected carefully upon the justice of their cause would have some reason to suppose that the membership in these two categories would overlap significantly.

At this point a significant difference should be noted between the punishment of corporations on the one hand and, on the other, terrorist activities against organized groups such as nation states. In both cases all the individual members of the collective in question may be considered vicariously responsible for the wrongful actions done by that collective, but the impact of the punishment of corporations differs significantly from the impact of terrorist activities against nation states, for example. Courts may (or may not) select fines or penalties that will affect some members of a corporation more severely than others. By contrast, terrorist activities directly affect individual members of the collective condemned by the terrorists. The point I wish to make is this: while the determination that an organized group is liable to various penalties is similar in the case of both the corporation and those groups that terrorists may condemn, the distribution of penalties will differ in important ways between the two. While courts may impose directly upon a corporation fines which will have an indirect, and varying, impact upon its members, terrorists with their limited numbers and resources will usually be able to have a direct impact only upon a few members of the group they oppose and an indirect impact upon the group as a whole. In general terrorism impacts directly upon individual members of a group, while by contrast court actions against corporations, and for that matter wars between nation states, have, as it were, an 'impersonal' quality about them which reflects the fact that organized groups are pitted against one another. Perhaps it is the personal and immediate nature of the threat that terrorism poses that accounts in part for the public outrage against it, an outrage which in terms of the actual harm that terrorists can do seems otherwise greatly exaggerated. Terrorism is often condemned as a threat to 'civilization' in a way that war and crime somehow are not, though they cause far more actual harm. Perhaps my point about how terrorists generally proceed against a group by attacking, sometimes randomly, its individual members will help to make public outrage against terrorism more intelligible. If what I have said is correct, it would follow that terrorists who wish to influence public opinion favorably on behalf of their cause will take care to be highly selective in their choice of targets. From both the moral and the prudential point of view, they should target only those individuals who can be shown to be directly at fault for the injustices done by the group the terrorists condemn.

Much, but not all, of what I have said above applies to the 'morally concerned' foes of terrorism as well, but with an important difference: the foes of terrorism in our world tend to be the leaders of rich and powerful nations which have it within their power to act directly against the groups or collectives that terrorists may in some sense be said to represent, or against 'host' communities or nations which permit terrorist organizations to exist within their jurisdiction. Powerful nation states which have grown impatient with continued terrorist activities and are convinced that the cause espoused by some particular terrorist organization(s) is without merit may be tempted to resort to a variety of activities, including all-out military attack, but there are often good reasons for these powerful nation states to exercise caution. First, there is the danger of overreaction, which may play into the terrorists' hands. Second, we need to bear in mind that, while terrorist organizations typically constitute a conspiracy, it may often be difficult to determine just how much support they are actually receiving from the larger group which they claim to represent or from the 'host' community from which they operate. Presumably even where there is evidence of significant support, not all the members of the group or community will be active participants. Here two analogies are relevant. In the case of a criminal conspiracy, for example to rob a bank, there may be people outside the gang who 'know what is going on' and offer support of various kinds. While some of this support may itself be considered criminal (see Chapter 1), the law may deal more leniently with these accomplices than with the actual members of the gang. In cases of criminal wrongdoing by a business conspiracy, as discussed in this and the preceding chapter, it may be the case that there are low-level management personnel and employees who know nothing of the activities in question, and I have argued that the courts should try to protect them as much as possible from the impact of fines or other penalties imposed on the corporation. These two analogies suggest that the foes of terrorism should be as selective as possible, endeavoring to limit their retaliations to terrorist organizations, and in some cases to their proven accomplices.

It may be recalled that in Chapter 1 I argued that while terrorism, where it is morally justifiable, should be as selective as possible, eventually terrorists might be justified in striking out at members of the 'silent majority' of a nation which had repeatedly ignored their demands for justice. However, where morally justifiable actions against terrorism are concerned things are somewhat more complicated. Because terrorist organizations are conspiracies, striking out against any of their members may, under certain circumstances, be warranted, but it is less clear whether striking out against the larger groups which terrorist organizations claim to represent, or their 'host' communities, would be morally warranted. Although things may change, terrorism thus far has simply not succeeded in becoming a major threat to the stability of any country. Israel may be a counter-example, though this seems doubtful, and, even if it were, many critics saw an alarming lack of proportion in the apparent willingness of Israel to destroy the entire city of Beirut in order to get at the PLO, even if this could have destroyed the PLO once and for all. Terrorists are desperate men, while their enemies (thus far) are more frustrated than desperate; this difference should seriously affect the range of options available, morally, to the respective parties.

One final note: it might be objected that I have 'saved' terrorism (in the sense of bestowing some limited moral respectability upon it in certain circumstances) only by assimilating it to something quite different, namely assassination. In so far as I have argued that terrorism should be as selective as possible, this is true, at least up to a point. The anarchist who assassinated President Garfield said that he did it in order to save the republic and to promote the sale of his book. If I am correct in my conception of what assassination involves, he could have assassinated the president solely in order to promote the sale of his book. The killing of a public official for any purpose, public (to save the republic) or private (to promote the sale of a book or to impress a young actress), is to be counted as assassination. But even if this is wrong, and assassination is possible only for public reasons, it still need not be linked to any effort to bring about political, social, economic, or religious change; that is, it can be done over an issue with no significant impact on public policy. Terrorism differs from assassination in being directed at influencing the behavior of groups, and this is true regardless of how selective it may be in the choice of targets. Thus, for terrorism there is a long list of considerations having to do with things such as group membership and vicarious liability which simply need not be relevant to a discussion of assassination. The morality of groups is necessarily an issue in the case of terrorism but not in the case of assassination.

Notes

Introduction

1 For a useful account of various definitions of terrorism, see Stephen Segaller, *Invisible Armies, Terrorism into the 1990's*, New York, 1987, pp. 7–25.

2 John Rawls, *A Theory of Justice*, Cambridge, Mass., 1971.

3 ibid.

4 Albert Camus, *The Rebel*, New York, 1967.

5 Bob Woodward, *Veil: The Secret Wars of the CIA 1981–1987*, New York, 1987, pp. 124–9.

6 Although terrorists seek publicity, it may not always further their ends. Publicity may focus entirely or mainly on the gory details of what the terrorists have done, without analyzing their motives or explaining their objectives. Even if the media do direct attention to the terrorists' cause, this does not, of course, guarantee a sympathetic response or any widespread belief that the terrorists' cause is a just one. Also, it may be that the terrorists will, as one critic has put it, fall in love with their own press clippings: 'Headlines became a substitute for truly meaningful grassroots political or military actions and gave PLO leaders a much exaggerated sense of their own strength' (Thomas L. Friedman, *From Beirut to Jerusalem*, New York, 1989, p. 124).

7 Benjamin Netanyahu, in *Terrorism. How the West Can Win* (ed. Benjamin Netanyahu, New York, 1986), dismisses

any connection between terrorism and the demand for justice: 'The root cause of terrorism lies not in grievances but in a disposition toward unbridled violence' (p. 204). He maintains that the root cause of terrorism is terrorists. John O'Sullivan in the same anthology writes that, 'A terrorist is a criminal who seeks publicity . . . . They *require* publicity' (p. 120). However, since criminals, with a few colourful exceptions (Bonnie and Clyde?) shun publicity, this should alert O'Sullivan to a significant difference between terrorists and criminals, and if he had explored the implications of his statement that they *require* publicity he (and Netanyahu) might have understood that the terrorists' need for publicity is linked not to their alleged criminality or their alleged disposition to violence but to their political agenda which requires publicity for their grievances.

8   Karl Popper, *The Open Society and its Enemies*, Princeton, 1945; Karl Popper, 'Utopia and violence,' in Joe White (ed.) *Assent/Dissent*, Dubuque, 1984, pp. 111–20.
9   J. W. N. Watkins, 'Methodological individualism and social tendencies,' *The British Journal for the Philosophy of Science* VIII (1957): 101–17.

1 Can terrorism be justifed?

1   R. M. Hare, 'On terrorism,' *Journal of Value Inquiry XIII* (Winter, 1979); Kai Nielsen, 'On terrorism and political assassination,' in Harold M. Zellner (ed.) *Assassination*, Cambridge, Mass., 1974.
2   Carl Wellman, 'On terrorism itself,' *Journal of Value Inquiry* XIII (Winter 1979): 250–8.
3   ibid., p. 255.
4   Joel Feinberg, 'Collective responsibility,' *Doing and Deserving*, Princeton, 1970.
5   Karl Jaspers, *The Question of German Guilt*, New York, 1947, p. 76. Earlier Jaspers wrote that 'there can be no collective guilt of a people or a group within a people –

except for political liability' (p. 42). But his subsequent judgment that 'there can be no radical separation of moral and political guilt' (p. 77) reflects his awareness of the intimacy of politics and morality and provides a basis for his own pronouncements concerning the collective political and moral guilt of the German people.

6   Feinberg, op. cit., p. 248.

7   Jaspers, op. cit., pp. 92–3.

8   It is arguable that state terrorism does not entirely fit my definition of terrorism. While it is aimed at bringing about political, social, economic, or religious change by the use of violence, it does not typically seek publicity for its goals or cause. Stephen Segaller in discussing 'state terror' speaks of acts of 'secret terror' by a government against some of its people, (*Invisible Armies. Terrorism into the 1990's*, New York, 1947, pp. 15–16). In the case of Germany, however, while the *details* of what the Nazis were doing were apparently not in the public domain, the fact that the government was acting against the Jews was not secret, nor was it meant to be. Typically state terrorism does not seek to provoke extreme counter-measures, though it may use such counter-measures to its own advantage, for example as a justification for severe reprisals. Lamentably enough, the practitioners of state terrorism all too often believe in the justice of their cause. On balance, I think we are warranted in classifying 'state terror' as a species of terrorism.

9   Arthur C. Danto, 'A logical portrait of the assassin,' and James Rachel, 'Political assassination,' in Zellner, op. cit.

10   Hare, op. cit.

2 Terrorism and consequentialism

1   R. M. Hare, 'What is wrong with slavery,' *Philosophy and Public Affairs* VIII (Winter, 1979): 103–21.

2   R. M. Hare, 'On terrorism,' *Journal of Value Inquiry* XIII (Winter, 1979): 243.

3   ibid., 244.

4   ibid., 245.

5   ibid., 247–8.

6   Other commentators share Hare's pessimism about what terrorism can accomplish. Senator Daniel Patrick Moynihan believes that when terrorism succeeds it results in totalitarianism: 'More or less uniformly, terrorism, when successful, ends in totalitarianism. The totalitarian state is terrorism came to power' ('Terrorists, totalitarians, and the rule of law' in Benjamin Netanyahu (ed.) *Terrorism. How the West Can Win*, New York, 1986, p. 41). Since Moynihan proceeds immediately to criticize Lenin's idea of an elite of 'vanguard fighters,' it may be that in speaking of successful terrorism he has in mind Lenin's Red Terror. However, Lenin's Red Terror was a means of helping to secure a totalitarian regime which was already in power. While some, perhaps many, terrorist groups are totalitarian to begin with, no essential connection between terrorism as I have defined it and totalitarianism exists; and indeed, terrorism may be directed against an oppressive totalitarian regime.

7   Kai Nielsen, 'On terrorism and political assassination,' in Harold M. Zellner (ed.) *Assassination*, Cambridge, Mass., 1974, pp. 97–8.

8   ibid., pp. 100–1.

9   Ted Honderich, 'Four conclusions about violence of the left,' *Canadian Journal of Philosophy* IX (June, 1979): 225–6.

10   ibid., 226.

11   ibid., 240.

12   ibid., 243.

13   ibid., 246.

3 Violence and force

1   Newton Garver, 'What violence is,' *The Nation*, June 24, 1968, 817–22.

2 ibid., 819.

3 Although we often speak of harm or injury as if they were identical, in the law we find that there may be a harm that is not an injury, as in harm to one's reputation, and an injury which is not a harm, as in injury which is inflicted upon a party with his consent. Historically 'injury' was used to refer to a wrong or rights violation, whereas 'harm' was used to refer to a damage or loss. The more prevalent modern usage is to use 'injury' to refer to physical harm, and 'harm' to refer to any set-back to an interest, regardless of whether it is a wrong or a rights violation. See Hyman Gross, *A Theory of Criminal Justice*, New York, 1979, pp. 115–22, and Joel Feinberg, *Harm to Others*, New York, 1984, pp. 32–6, 106–7. However, Feinberg's proposed 'harm principle' involves 'harm' both in the sense of a set-back to an interest and in the sense of a wrong or injustice.

4 Burleigh Taylor Wilkins and Kelly Zelikovitz, 'Principles for individual actions,' *Philosophia* 14 (1984): 299–319.

5 See Herbert Morris, 'Persons and punishment,' *The Monist* 52 (1968): 475–501.

6 See Joel Feinberg, 'The nature and value of rights,' *Rights, Justice, and the Bounds of Liberty*, Princeton, 1980, pp. 149–53. Morris and Feinberg take the line that the notion of a prima facie right makes little sense or is absurd. Morris writes (op. cit., 499): 'If we begin to think that the right itself is prima facie, we shall in cases in which we are justified in not according it, fail sufficiently to bring out that we have interfered where justice says we should not.' But in cases where we are justified in not according a man his rights, why wouldn't justice say we have interfered where we should have interfered? The historic distinction between the possession of a right and its exercise might prove helpful here: a man may possess the prima-facie right to x but if he violates certain conditions he will not be allowed to exercise this right.

7   Richard Kraut, *Socrates and the State*, Princeton, 1984, p. 104.
8   Quoted by Stephen Segaller, *Invisible Armies. Terrorism in the 1990's*, New York, 1947, pp. 106–7.
9   Larry May in *The Morality of Groups*, Notre Dame, 1987, pp. 156–78, argues that the rights of disadvantaged individuals should take precedence over the rights of advantaged individuals, especially when their disadvantages are 'group-based.' May has in mind things like the rights of racial minorities to file class action suits in the courts in matters involving discrimination, but I can see in his argument reasons why he might be somewhat sympathetic to what I am saying here.
10   See John Rawls, *A Theory of Justice*, Cambridge, Mass., 1971, pp. 54–117, 258–332.

4 Innocence, just wars, and terrorism

1   Civil wars are harder to characterize, but they seem to fall somewhere between war and revolution. They may, for example, be wars of territorial secession, like the American Civil War, in which case they seem more like wars; or they may be wars of civil or religious strife, as in Lebanon, in which case they seem more like revolutions.

2   Nevertheless, where terrorism is concerned the problem of legitimacy does pose some interesting questions. Is it possible, for example, for a group of students to 'represent' the working class and to perform terrorist acts on its behalf? Suppose there are no ties whatever, no economic, cultural, or religious connections, between terrorists and their alleged constituency: is a disinterested terrorism prompted solely by a burning, or fanatical, passion for justice possible? Perhaps it is. Here one might say that the terrorists, although not the chosen representatives of their 'constituency,' can nevertheless represent its interests, and thus preserve, however tenuously, some claim to legitimacy. But this leads directly to the question of the attitude

'the constituency' may take toward what is being done on its behalf. To do violence on behalf of a people or group who expressly and freely reject such violence would surely count as an example of paternalism of the most odious sort.

3   James Turner Johnson's *Just War Tradition and the Restraint of War*, Princeton, 1981, is a useful account of just war doctrine.

5 Responsibility for the My Lai Massacre

1   See Seymour Hersh, *My Lai 4: A Report on the Massacre and Its Aftermath*, New York, 1970; Richard Hammer, *The Court-Martial of Lt. Calley*, New York, 1971; and Telford Taylor, *Nuremberg and Vietman: An American Tragedy*, New York, 1970.

2   Cooper's 'Responsibility and the "system" ' is in an excellent collection of essays by philosophers, most of whom had previously written on collective responsibility, in which they attempt to examine the My Lai Massacre in the light of their theories: Peter French (ed.) *Individual and Collective Responsibility: Massacre at My Lai*, Cambridge, Mass., 1972. I recommend all the essays, but especially those by Kurt Baier, Virginia Held, and H. D. Lewis.

3   David Cooper, 'Collective responsibility,' *Philosophy* XLIII (July, 1968): 260.

4   Joel Feinberg, 'Collective responsibility,' *Doing and Deserving*, Princeton, 1970.

5   See Virginia Held, 'Can a random collection of individuals be morally responsible?' *Journal of Philosophy* LXVII (July 23, 1970): 471–81, and also her 'Moral responsibility and collective action,' in French, op cit., pp. 103–30.

6   Cooper, 'Responsibility and the "system",' in French, op. cit., pp. 87–9.

7   ibid., p. 92.

8 ibid., p. 95.
9 ibid., p. 96–7.
10 ibid., p. 97.
11 ibid., p. 99–100.
12 ibid., p. 100.
13 See M. Patricia Roth, *The Juror and the General*, New York, 1986, for an interesting account by a juror of the famous libel trial of *Westmorland v. CBS* over CBS's controversial documentary, *The Uncounted Enemy: A Vietnam Deception*. Westmoreland simply did not include guerrillas, the Self-Defense force, and the Secret Self-Defense force in his estimates of Viet Cong operating in South Vietnam.
14 Seymour Hersh, *Cover-Up*, New York, 1972, p. 234. No investigation was ever made of a massacre by Bravo Company which allegedly killed at least sixty civilians at My Lai 1 on the very morning that Charlie Company went into My Lai 4. Both companies were participants in the same operation.

6 The responsibility of corporations

1 Peter A. French, *Collective and Corporate Responsibility*, New York, 1984, *passim*.
2 Jean-Paul Sartre, *Critique of Dialectical Reason*, London, 1976; Larry May, *The Morality of Groups*, Notre Dame, 1987, pp. 33–41, 58–65, 73–83. J. W. N. Watkins' 'Methodological individualism and social tendencies' is the classic formulation of methodological individualism where the philosophy of social science and history is concerned. See *The British Journal for the Philosophy of Science* VIII (1957): 101–17.
3 May, op. cit., p. 66.
4 ibid., p. 80.
5 ibid., p. 22.
6 ibid., p. 46.

7 Alvin Goldman, 'Toward a theory of social power,' *Philosophical Studies*, 23 (1972): 234–41.

8 May, op. cit., p. 48.

9 ibid., pp. 65, 66.

10 ibid., pp. 69–70.

11 Angelo Corlett, 'Corporate responsibility and punishment,' *Public Affairs Quarterly* II (1988): 1–16; Victor Tam, 'May on corporate responsibility and punishment,' *Business and Professional Ethics* VIII (1990): 65–81.

12 Joel Feinberg, 'Collective responsibility,' *Doing and Deserving*, Princeton, 1970.

13 May, op. cit., p. 85.

14 ibid., p. 99.

15 ibid., p. 84.

16 ibid., pp. 86–7.

17 ibid., p. 99.

18 ibid., pp. 104–5.

19 ibid., p. 42.

20 ibid., p. 101.

21 ibid.

7 The distribution of liability

1 Joel Feinberg, 'Collective responsibility,' *Doing and Deserving*, Princeton, 1970, p. 249.

2 Larry May, *The Morality of Groups*, Notre Dame, 1987.

3 ibid., p. 94.

Index